The Missing Risk Premium

Why Low Volatility Investing Works

Eric G. Falkenstein

ISBN: 1470110970
ISBN 13: 9781470110970

Table of Contents

I.	Chapter I: Introduction	I
2:	Chapter 2: Asset Pricing Theory	9
	2.1 *Utility Functions*	9
	2.2 *Diversification and the Efficient Frontier*	11
	2.3 *Tobin's Separation Theorem*	12
	2.4 *The Capital Asset Pricing Model (CAPM)*	14
	2.5 *Arbitrage Pricing Theory and Stochastic Discount Factors*	16
3	The Rise and Fall of Standard Models	21
	3.1 *Early Tests of the CAPM*	21
	3.2 *Later Tests of the CAPM*	24
	3.3 *APT Tests*	26
	3.4 *Fama and French (1992) Change the Debate*	29
	3.5 *The Current Standard Model*	31
	3.6 *Serial Changes to the APT*	33
4:	A Survey of Empirical Evidence	35
	4.1 *Volatility and Cross-Sectional Equity Returns*	36
	4.2 *Minimum-Variance Portfolios*	39
	4.3 *Beta*	41
	4.4 *Distress Risk*	44
	4.5 *Leverage and Returns*	46
	4.6 *Penny Stocks*	47
	4.7 *Equity Options*	47
	4.8 *Initial Public Offerings and Seasoned Equity Offerings*	49
	4.9 *Analyst Disagreement*	50
	4.10 *Mutual Funds*	51
	4.11 *Volatility over Time*	52
	4.12 *Overnight versus Intraday Equity Returns*	55
	4.13 *World Returns*	58
	4.14 *Equity Risk Premium*	59
	4.15 *Entrepreneurial Investments*	68
	4.16 *Private Equity*	69
	4.17 *Currencies*	71
	4.18 *Corporate Bonds*	74
	4.19 *Yield Curve*	77

4.20	Futures	80
4.21	Movies	82
4.22	Sports Books	83
4.23	Lotteries	84
4.24	Real Estate	85
4.25	Hedge Funds and CTAs	86
4.26	Summary	87
5: Relative Status Utility and Risk Premiums		89
5.1	The General Theory of Relative Status Asset Pricing	90
5.2	Equilibrium with Relative Utility	91
5.3	Arbitrage with Relative Utility	94
5.4	The Low Return to High-Risk Assets	98
5.5	Academic Precedence	99
5.6	Uncertainty and Fat Tails	102
6: Why Envy Explains More than Greed		105
6.1	Robust Hard Wiring	105
6.2	The Easterlin Paradox	110
6.3	Politics of Envy	111
6.4	Benchmarking	112
6.5	Virtue Always in Moderation	113
6.6	Conclusion	117
7: Why We Take Too Much Financial Risk		119
7.1	Investors Ignoring the Standard Theory	121
7.2	Winner's Curse	123
7.3	Overconfidence	125
7.4	Risk-Loving Preferences	126
7.5	Information Costs	128
7.6	Alpha Discovery	129
7.7	Representativeness Bias	129
7.8	Convex Payoffs to Professionals	130
7.9	Conclusion	130
8: Why This Bad Theory Is So Popular		133
8.1	Moralistic Fallacy	133
8.2	Wrong for a Long Time	134
8.3	Sophisticated Analysis	137
8.4	Epilogue: My Anecdote	138
9: Practical Implications		141
9.1	Low-Volatility Investing	141
9.2	A Mid Beta Portfolio	144
9.3	Sundry	145
10: Conclusion		151
Bibliography		155
Notes		163

"It doesn't matter how beautiful your theory is, it doesn't matter how smart you are. If it doesn't agree with experiment, it's wrong."

—RICHARD FEYNMAN

"The opposite of courage in our society is not cowardice, it is conformity."

—ROLLO MAY

"...rank among our equals, is, perhaps, the strongest of all our desires."

—ADAM SMITH

Preface

This book outlines an important flaw in finance and the academic notion of risk. It gets into how the original asset pricing model went wrong, why it is empirically bankrupt, why people continue to believe it, and why my approach is better. It is most relevant to students, financial professionals, and anyone interested in what social scientists mean by "risk."

Risk and return are presumably two sides of the same coin, and because risk is a covariance, something objective, one presumably can estimate the risk, determine the expected returns, and then lay one's chips around the table appropriately. The theory makes complete sense to economists who, not coincidentally, are relatively good at the kind of analytic problem they think completely describes the investment problem. Yet something clearly seems wrong.

One prominent signal comes from the market for financial professionals at hedge funds, where pre-fees at least, they clearly have the most alpha in the industry. Most funds are interested in hiring people who merely have quantitative or programming skills and are completely uninterested in economists who understand utility functions, stochastic discount functions, Euler equations, generalized method of moments, and other tools that are the *sine qua non* of academic economics and finance. In practical finance, a computer science or physics PhD is generally more attractive than an economics or finance PhD mainly because that person knows more programming, which *is* useful. More important, a finance PhD will lead to an emphasis on covariances, and the translation of volatility into expected returns, or statistical techniques that find patterns that can't be translated into simple scatter plots, all poor intuition when looking for useful solutions. If you want to teach and publish academic papers, modern asset pricing theory is very useful, but it has about as much relevance as *Das Kapital* to any practitioner. If risk premiums were really ubiquitous, finance-specific tools would be valuable to hedge funds. They are not and this highlights their irrelevancy.

I've been actively employed in finance for over twenty years, and the big decisions are not close to being described using modern finance. For example, my first trade ever was a put on the S&P 100 back on October 16, 1987, which turned $2,860 into $41,122 when I sold it the following Monday.[1] That's a 1,438 percent return. Over the next few months, I decided I would use options to take advantage of my belief that the market would rebound. I placed market orders for options on individual stocks and discovered the commission greatly underestimated total trading expenses, as the bid-ask spread back then was about 30 percent. Then I had to pay about 30 percent on my 1987 capital gains, so by October 1988, after not many trades, I was net dollar flat, though my arithmetic average return was still north of 1000 percent, and my general market call correct. Everyone recommended that I not mention my losses in applying to graduate school, only my winning trade.

My experience was not an exception, but rather, typical. One should not place market orders in illiquid markets, or to take a more parochial example, buy the VXX for volatility insurance when the VIX futures curve is in strong contango.[2] The survivorship reporting bias I was encouraged to apply, meanwhile, is a mainstay in the finance industry where most extant funds somehow manage to beat their 5-year Lipper Averages. Understanding that finance is not primarily based on the standard notion of risk is like when learning that Yahoo! is not so much a tech company as much as an advertising company; it changes a lot. The risk premium emphasis of modern finance is not helpful to someone trying to truly understand this field.

The essence of financial wisdom is best reflected by a small set of principles. Aside from derivatives pricing models and efficient markets, which I think of as separate principles that are quite useful, the main ideas from modern asset pricing theory are the following: the quantity of risk is measured by a covariance with priced risk factors which are as-yet unidentified time series *like* the stock market, and there's a linear relation between this risk metric and expected returns. These are not in the top three things I want my son to understand when he becomes an adult. That is, the first key to investing is an understanding of history that comes from reading various accounts of the internet bubble or the conglomerate boom of the 1960's. Secondly, I would emphasize that finance is as much about personal relationships as it is about objective patterns, so find mentors and colleagues and try to help them so they will someday feel inclined to help you. Thirdly, that investing is like any other endeavor, where above average performance depends on some kind of edge, so if you have no reason to presume you have an edge assume it is negative and invest in assets where this hurts you the least. Risk premiums are a distraction.

A good example of the contrast between theory and practice comes from Long Term Capital Management (LTCM), the famed hedge fund that imploded in 1998. In theory, when it was working, outsiders thought they were using computer models to implement highfalutin theoretical insights from their two eminent financial theorists, Nobel Laureates Robert Merton and Myron Scholes. In practice, they put on some simple trades that were neither clever nor subtle, as they failed primarily due to a failed interest rate bet and a bet on volatility. Merton and Scholes were irrelevant to the investment decisions throughout, yet they were disingenuously presented for marketing the fund. That is the essence of modern finance: a rigorous, disingenuous façade, and a seat-of-the-pants practical side.

In the standard model, intelligence has absolutely nothing to do with investment success, and some papers actually suggest the rich are stupid because they contain a disproportionate number of lucky morons who did not realize they were taking as much risk as there were, as would be the case if riches generally came from lotteries.[3] In fact, the main investment issues are navigating a world with complex tax codes and lots of objectively bad investments that try to mislead ignorant investors. For example, wealth management officers target clients with $5MM or more in assets, and the primary knowledge of these people is inheritance and tax law. Discussion of the most elementary mathematics—standard deviations—is done with moderation. This makes sense because discussion of mathematics, as applied to finance, does tend to become excessively pretentious, pedantic, and irrelevant, and is primarily used, like Merton and Scholes for the failed LTCM, for impressing and intimidating the many mediocre people who can be intimidated by credentials and math.

We should all strive for something better than the misleading usage of risk to conceal one's true actions, unless you aspire to be a shill. Risk has become a concept like diversity or the Trinity, words that are either used by confused people of good faith certain that any inconsistency comes from insufficient understanding, or simple hucksters who use it as a red herring.[4]

Moderation is the key to all things good and so too with mathematics. I do not think that one needs to understand graduate level mathematics to understand any good financial idea. I also think that a basic understanding of algebra and statistics is essential for many good financial ideas. I try to keep the more extended algebraic derivations in endnotes because while they are not necessary for understanding my arguments, they are useful for the reader who wants a deeper understanding. I could not outline my new approach without algebra, however, though math phobic readers can skip the sections with equations and still get the gist of my new approach. Those who think 'history is bunk' can skip chapters 2 and 3.

Though I am a critic of standard approaches, I find myself generally agreeing with economists who represent these approaches more than their critics. That is, the most common criticisms of modern financial theory are based on the argument that markets are irrational or inefficient, with reference to behavioral finance and systematic biases. This highlights that it is not sufficient to note the current status quo is wrong but in precisely what way because this matters. As mentioned, the theory of efficient markets and derivatives pricing theory are to my mind very useful and unrelated to the main problem in finance. It is essential to address best arguments of your adversaries, so I try to present the standard model sympathetically. As for references of the theory and data I am addressing, I suggest two survey books over any others: Mark Rubinstein's *A History of the Theory of Investments* and Antti Ilmanen's *Expected Returns*. The standard model I allude to in this book is exemplified by popular MBA and graduate level textbooks, such as Brealey and Myers's *Principles of Corporate Finance* and John Cochrane's *Asset Pricing*.

CHAPTER 1

Introduction

Modern portfolio theory is a framework that holds that the expected return of a financial asset is a function of risk, where you are paid to endure this unpleasant, irreducible characteristic. This idea has so many interested constituencies that it's as though a conspiracy were acting to keep everyone from noticing that the riskiest investments are not those with the highest expected returns but rather like lottery tickets catering to the deluded.

The vested interests in the current paradigm of asset pricing theory include many different groups that have various reasons to tendentiously filter reality. Economists love it because it implies and is implied by one of the most fundamental assumptions in economics, so its existence is necessary for thousands of papers to be relevant.[5] Investment managers like it because they need only point to "risk" as why their returns have been above average. If risk—and thus return—is a choice, you can do it again and, given the state of this theory, not have to explain what risk actually is. Hucksters like it because it conveniently detracts investors from monitoring hidden costs and fraud, which are rampant in finance. Pension administrators like it because it rationalizes asset returns well above the risk-free rate, which reduces your need for more funding. Finance professors like it because it generates a consistent and rigorous sequence of lectures that all build upon each other, as any decent science should, and underlies a methodology mastery that defines its reputation. One could go on and on.

There is no shortage of people believing the standard theory is true because of its convenient implications.

When finance created asset pricing theory in the 1950s and '60s, the rational reductionism underlying the standard model was moving through much of the social sciences, as it seemed obvious that applying logic would render previously intractable, qualitative problems into unambiguous solutions within the new disciplines of dynamic programming or game theory. The solution of "how to invest" seemed just around the corner. Seminal work by Markowitz, Tobin, and Sharpe created modern portfolio theory and the capital asset pricing model (CAPM) with its "betas."[6] Around that same time this was completed, researchers at the University of Chicago documented that the aggregate stock indexes had generated a sizable 5 percent return premium over treasury bills for the period 1926–1962, which seemed to confirm the existence of a fact predicted by the theory.[7]

The basic idea of how the risk premium works is the following. An asset's price is the present value of future payoffs, where the discount rate is the risk factor. Equation 1.1 shows a pricing function for a simple security with one payout or future value in consideration. This expected future value is then discounted by the gross expected return.

$$Price = \frac{E(FutureValue)}{1+r+g} \tag{1.1}$$

Here r is a risk-free interest rate, and g is the risk premium. So r today would be a number like 0.04, and g, perhaps 0.035. The risk premium is an unobserved variable that connects the expected future payoff to the current price, and so price movements are often explained in terms of changes in risk (though the expected future values are also clearly volatile). Note that the discount rate and expected return are really different terms here for the same thing, the denominator here, one going from future value to present value, and the other the reverse. The risk premium, g, is a function of a covariance with something like the S&P 500 stock index (e.g., contained in the CAPM beta) and then multiplied by the corresponding risk factor premia (e.g., the equity risk premium).

By 1971, the earliest version of the theory was so dominant it appeared on a cover story for *Institutional Investor Magazine*—"The Beta Cult: The New Way to Measure Risk"—and when a couple of early papers seemed to confirm the theory a couple years later the CAPM achieved primacy in asset pricing theory.[8] Although the original CAPM has been replaced by a framework, it retains the same essential qualities of the CAPM. The keys are risk aversion over aggregate wealth, risk measured as the covariance of the asset with the risk factors, and a linear price for risk (twice the risk generates twice the excess return).[9] The covariance of the asset with the factor is the quantity of risk, whereas the price of risk is reflected by the expected return of that factor (e.g., the difference in the S&P 500 over the risk-free rate).

The academic history of risk is usually presented as the crowning success story of the social sciences, with its cannon of heroes from Nobelists Harry Markowitz to Danny Kahneman. The story of the standard financial model was presented in a bestseller by Peter Bernstein titled *Against the Odds: The Remarkable Story of Risk*, where Bernstein chronicled the development of the standard model from the middle ages, and noted that

> By showing the world how to understand risk, measure it, and weigh its consequences, they converted risk-taking into one of the prime catalysts that drives Western society. Like Prometheus, they defied the gods and probed the darkness in search of the light that converted the future from an enemy into an opportunity.[10]

It's a very attractive story, the kind Malcolm Gladwell writes about upstarts who turn over paradigms with their unique genius. The problem is, there's no evidence for the theory Bernstein so exuberantly praised. As Mark Rubinstein said about the CAPM and its extensions, "More empirical effort may have been put into testing the CAPM equation than any other result in finance. The results are quite mixed and in many ways discouraging."[11] Eugene Fama and Kenneth French called the CAPM "empirically vacuous," whereas Stephen Ross noted that "having a low, middle or high beta does not matter; the expected return is the same."[12] And these are major proponents of the current paradigm.

If a Martian looked at the data, he would have to say that as a first-order approximation, asset pricing theory has the wrong sign. Below I survey twenty-five asset classes, and generally the result is no relation, then a negative correlation, and finally a couple consistent with the theory. This pattern is typical, and I could go on and list a dozen more cases because the truth has a lot of implications. No other article, paper, or book puts all this evidence together, primarily because no one thinks this general absence of a positive risk-return relation implies it might not actually be there. It's a bit like nineteenth-century physicists who assumed the luminiferous aether was present and kept coming up with more fanciful explanations for why it couldn't be measured.[13] It turned out there was no aether.

Although many have emphasized that empirical failure is caused by the subtlety of risk and expected return, consider beauty, which like risk in that it is omnipresent and subjective. Psychologists can objectively identify characteristics of beauty across cultures: things related to fertility like smooth skin, symmetric face, and for women a 0.7 hip-to-waist ratio.[14] Similar quantification has been applied to the beauty of voices. If some subjective preference truly exists among humans, it can be quantified and agree with intuition.

In contrast, risk has devolved into something like Freud's Oedipal complex, where a young boy presumably wishes to have sex with his mother and fears castration from his father, and this causes all sorts of issues. Most people find this absurd, but if you have ever met someone who invested in psychoanalysis, that person will just tell you the theory is much more subtle, so much so it is clearly nonfalsifiable and thus unhelpful for anything but rationalizing. Similarly, a company like Coca-Cola has high profitability, low volatility, low leverage, low beta, and a higher return than a comparably large company like the old General Motors that went bankrupt had, which for decades had low profitability, high volatility, high leverage, high beta but ultimately went bankrupt. The point is not those two particular companies but rather companies with characteristics like Coca-Cola's seem safe, and they have higher returns than companies like GM have, which seem risky. The current paradigm wants you to think that GM-type companies are not risky, as evidenced by their lower average returns, and Coca-Cola-type companies are risky, as evidenced by their higher average returns. It's possible this is all the result of emergent properties one does not see from the bottom up, and that the raw data gloss over some underlying subtlety that is totally consistent with an intuitive manifestation of risk, but I am very skeptical. This is hardly the organized common sense that presumably describes any successful social science. It defies credulity that the solution to this empirical pattern is within the standard paradigm.

The standard theory assumes people are paid to withstand an objective undesirable, like receiving a dollar for every extra minute you leave your hand in hot water—those who have the highest pain tolerance achieve the highest returns on average.[15] Yet in practice, onerous or smelly jobs usually pay poorly, as any toilet cleaner knows, because too many are willing to submit themselves to large amounts of unpleasantness for higher rewards.[16]

Why is this important? Risk taking is a key life skill, so understanding how it pays off is important. The idea that to get rich you need to take risk seems to imply that risk begets higher returns, but this is just a logical fallacy, like using successful gamblers as role models for investing.[17] Further, a great deal of time is wasted on risk premiums that do not exist because, like Freudian psychoanalysis, there is a large erudite and energetic set of true believers and much material to rationalize any observation within the paradigm. Alas, investing is much less rigorous, but much more difficult, than what is implied via the standard theory.

The idea that financial courage produces a strictly increasing and linear expected payoff to risk bearing is contrary to the payoffs to every virtue, which all require moderation and trade-offs with competing virtues. Oxygen, radiation, vitamin A but also politeness, loyalty, and honesty all are detrimental at levels too small or too large. Courage is productive only if tempered with prudence, which takes into account one's special capabilities for one's opportunities; there is no linear "courage premium." A theory that implies a ubiquitous linear payoff to an action like exposure to volatility, regardless of context or quantity, would be unprecedented.

These basic assumptions about utility imply average investment returns should be a linear, positive function of risk, whereas in practice any measure of risk is at best uncorrelated with average returns and is often negative. Although this empirical finding has become accepted over the past twenty years, the academy has been quick to amend its previous theory with a simple addendum: risk is really subtle, multidimensional, and *sometimes* people are risk loving in *some* areas that turn risk premiums from positive to negative. In the words of leading research John Campbell, giving his overview of the state of finance at the Millennia, "Precisely because the conditions for the existence of a stochastic discount factor are so general, they place almost no restrictions on financial data."[18] The effect of a good theory is to make an accurate view of the world less complicated, not more, but instead modern researchers focus on the framework's potential and its usefulness for *post hoc* rationalization.

Most professors still teach the standard capital asset pricing model even though they know it does not work. It is pedagogically convenient, amenable to step-by-step derivations, and thus a series of lectures and homework assignments. They can justify this because they are confident that whatever form the final theory takes, it will embody its essential qualities of factor loadings from covariances (the how much of risk), a risk premium on that factor (its price), and a resulting linear relation between risk and expected return.[19]

If there is no risk premium, one of our most fundamental assumptions must not be true because the logic of the main theory has been exhaustively examined for decades, and it is not that there's a math error in the derivation from assumptions. There is just one necessary and sufficient condition for the existence of a risk premium: standard utility functions, which assume that our happiness is solely dependent on our individual wealth and increases at a decreasing rate. Clearly this idea applies to things like ice cream, in that I enjoy ice cream independent of others and less so the more I eat, but to extrapolate this to my entire wealth bundle is an error of significance.

If people are primarily envious, as opposed to greedy, the same logic that generates a positive risk premium generates a zero risk premium. A simple way to see this is to consider that if your benchmark is cash, then minimizing risk is to put your money in zero-returning cash; if your benchmark is the average return of your peers, then the risk-minimizing strategy is to do what everyone else is doing. In the relative wealth case, risk taking is symmetric—it can be too little or too much relative to the consensus, and due to arbitrage, there is no general risk premium in these cases.

Although most of us don't like to think we are driven by envy, most admit benchmarking against the consensus which is really just a semantic difference; indeed, they seem blithely ignorant of this inconsistency with their fundamental assumptions. Consider the vanguard of conventional academic financial wisdom, Eugene Fama, who described his foray into small-cap stocks as experiencing a "depression" in the late 1980s, when, in fact, it was only true on a *relative* basis. These depressed stocks were up 50 percent from 1985–1989, which is pretty high compared to other periods.[20] It's the return relative to the benchmark that is important, even for those pushing the standard theory.

Replacing "greed" with "envy" explains a lot more of the data. As hope exalts courage, the hope intrinsic to lottery-type returns creates foolhardy courage and explains their perversely poor returns. Equilibria where such effects exist are much more plausible in a relative risk model than in the standard model, where presumably most people would actively avoid index funds that necessarily contain these lousy stocks. This assumption is more consistent with a variety of other facts, such as that happiness does not increase as societies get wealthier, that all investments are sold with purported above-average returns, or that people invest too much in their home country. These all make sense if we are constantly benchmarking against our peers but instead are anomalies to the standard theory.

Unfortunately, driven in part by academic theory, too many investors naively think that merely taking risk generates the payoff for such risk, which discourages the follow-up that makes risk taking productive. Investing is like poker, where you have objective odds, asymmetric information and game-theoretic behavior. A good player is always thinking about what the other players are thinking, and this should be no less true when positioning one's 401k. You have to be disciplined and savvy to avoid the many investment advisers promoting bad gambles, taking advantage of the delusions and ignorance of most investors. It is not as if most investors are choosing between index funds; many if not most financial risk taking is more unconventional and costly (e.g., only about one out of fifty internet-based work-at-home business propositions are legitimate).[21]

Taken broadly, there is little evidence of a financial risk premium, yet the main datum for it remains the equity risk premium—the difference between the return on equities and the risk-free rate. This is a good example of why no theory is consistent with all the facts, because all the facts aren't true. I argue the average equity return is actually the risk-free rate because top-line returns assume investors are low-transaction, steady purchasers of low-cost indices, ignoring the taxes, market timing, transaction costs, geometric averaging, and survivorship bias that for most investors are far from trivial. For example, the best study of actual returns of individual investors is from DALBAR, a research firm that provides research for financial professionals about investor behavior. Each year, they publish a report called the *Quantitative Analysis of Investor Behavior* that compares the returns from average individual investors to various benchmarks using data from the Investment Company Institute.[22] The report documents that for the twenty years ending December 31, 2010, the S&P 500 annual return was 9.1 percent, whereas the average equity mutual fund investor generated only a return of 3.3 percent. That's a 5.8 percent gap, which is above almost all current estimates of the equity risk premium. The index returns are like the blackjack house take when players bet optimally, which would not be an equilibrium without the many drunk, ignorant, and impatient players who bet suboptimally.

Although broad asset indexes contain the wisdom of crowds, they also necessarily contain a lot of foolishness that make them distinctly suboptimal portfolios. Whereas you can find smart, educated people with opinions on any side of a debate, making it difficult to uncover the smart money, the stupid money is much more identifiable—they're into lottery tickets hoping to get rich quick with no effort. The effect is for really high-risk investments to have the most delusional investors, the most opportunistic sellers, and pathetic returns. This would be a mere curiosity if the indexes did not indiscriminately weight equities regardless of this attribute. By ridding your asset classes of these objectively bad assets, you can improve your returns rather simply, and this has been demonstrated in real time via the dominance of low-volatility investing.

A valuable takeaway comes merely from understanding that risk taking in investments is no different than risk taking in other dimensions of your life, something you apply in concert with your comparative advantage and in the right context. To the extent you take a risk without any specialized knowledge, expect to pay a price for the chutzpah of expecting to be rewarded for your hubris.

CHAPTER 2

Asset Pricing Theory

To understand the risk conundrum we are in it is necessary to understand the current theory. As the current theory is empirically vacuous—even to its most esteemed proponents—clearly it must have some attractive qualities outside its predictive ability.[23] Standard asset pricing theory comes out of rather innocuous-seeming assumptions, and is an application of pure logic to those assumptions. This chapter outlines the creation of standard theory. It is important to realize that it really derives from two pillars. First is the diminishing marginal utility of absolute wealth, a necessary and sufficient condition for generating a risk premium. The other pillar is the statistics of portfolios, the key being the idea that idiosyncratic volatility diversifies away. With these two key insights, the model follows rather trivially.

CAPM's amenability to a sequence of lectures and problem sets is definitely a major reason it remains popular. Using seemingly unimpeachable assumptions, you logically proceed to pricing implications, each step involving some clever mathematics or statistics, references to now-famous academics. Whatever its faults, such as being empirically vacuous, it is a wonderful theory to design a course around.

2.1 Utility Functions

In 1947, Johnny von Neumann and Oscar Morgenstern wrote *The Theory of Games and Economic Behavior*. Von Neumann was a mathematician who had earlier axiomatized set theory and quantum mechanics, so when economist Oscar Morgenstern pulled him in to help write a book on two-person zero-sum games like poker, von Neumann was the perfect person for generating assumptions that enabled the construction of a formal system whose consistency and completeness could be rigorously proven. He created a set of axioms that defined how such players evaluated random payoffs that they would apply to their parochial problem of zero-sum games.[24] The "von Neumann-Morgenstern utility function" was incidental, yet ultimately the most important contribution within their opus, and became the workhorse of economic models for the remainder of the century because a modeler could count on them having nice, consistent properties that were rigorously proven.

More important, von Neumann-Morgenstern applied their utility function to gamblers in games of poker, so it was pretty straightforward to apply this idea from one's gambling stake to one's total wealth. The risk aversion for someone managing a gambling pot seemed just like the risk aversion one has when looking at an entire bank account and thus wealth broadly defined. This was done immediately by Milton Friedman and Leonard J. Savage (1948), who used a von Neumann-Morgenstern utility function to expose the concept of univariate risk aversion. They noted that in the normal area of a utility curve, the utility of getting $2 for certain is higher than the utility of getting either $1 or $3 with a 50 percent probability.

FIGURE 2.1. *Utility as a function of wealth*

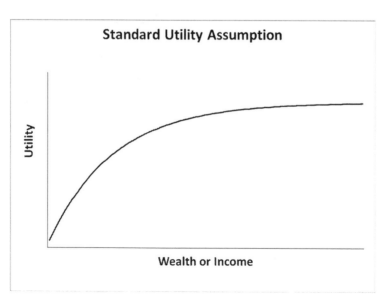

The implication of a function like Figure 2.1 is our common notion of risk aversion, as it shows utility increasing everywhere in wealth, though at a lower rate the wealthier you are. In such a scenario, individuals prefer a certain expected value to any gamble of that same expected value. Arrow (1965) showed that a risky asset must have a higher return than the risk-free rate—otherwise, no one would hold it, implying the market risk premium is greater than zero.

While many researchers looked at various utility specifications, in general, researchers considered the mean-variance preferences implied by:

$$U(x) = E(x) - a \cdot Var(x) \qquad (2.1)$$

That is, the expected utility of some payout x is a function of the expected payoff minus some constant a times the expected variance. Though mean-variance utility does not generalize well, it's a serviceable approximation, especially for expositing fundamental ideas.[25] As with the assumption about asset returns being normally distributed, which is also "wrong," this particular assumption is innocuous in most applications and incredibly easier to work with.

2.2 Diversification and the Efficient Frontier

The basic insights of Markowitz are intellectually satisfying because they are at once so simple and intuitive yet mathematically complicated. The basic idea is "don't put all your eggs in one basket."[26] Clearly, the idea of diversification did not originate with Markowitz—the concept having been mentioned in the Bible and Shakespeare and as a cliché mentioned in the 1940 investment classic *Where Are the Customer's Yachts?*—but Markowitz proved how assets should not be viewed by themselves but rather in the context of a portfolio when one is risk averse in the sense of Friedman and Savage.[27] Idiosyncratic risk, or risk unrelated to all the other assets, disappears in a portfolio, leaving only systematic or nondiversifiable volatility. This irreducible portfolio volatility is the only risk left.

Markowitz created the now standard method of graphing a set of assets in volatility-return space, where volatility is on the x-axis, and return is on the y-axis (he later wished he had volatility on the y-axis, and I concur, but such is path dependence). There is a hyperbola around these assets that represent all the various combinations of each asset, potential portfolios, with their various return and volatilities, and it curves because the covariance of the two assets makes their combination effect nonlinear.

FIGURE 2.2. *The efficient frontier*

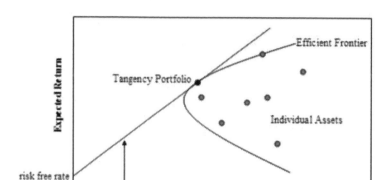

The portfolios on the upper part of this set of possible portfolios are called efficient portfolios because you can't achieve higher return without adding to portfolio volatility. Much of Markowitz's early writings involved a considerable amount of vector mathematics applied to statistics, mainly in outlining how to determine those portfolios on the efficient frontier, which given the complete set of assets in the universe, looks like the convex hull around the set of portfolio points above. Actually calculating the weightings of assets that define each point on the curved line is quite difficult, but this turned out to not matter. Interestingly, at this early stage, risk and portfolio standard deviation were synonymous.

2.3 Tobin's Separation Theorem

James Tobin (1958) found that if you throw in one "safe" asset with zero volatility, you get a neat result: the optimal portfolio in return-volatility space consists of one common portfolio representing all of the risky assets and various proportions of the safe asset. The idea is the most complicated, conceptually, in the development of the standard model. Start with the fact that investors are seeking to maximize return and minimize variance, so-called mean-variance preferences. These create a series of convex curves that do not cross, each consistent with some risk parameter a in the utility assumption $U(x)=E(x) - a \cdot Var(x)$. Now take a point on the y-axis, representing the risk-free rate R_f. If you extend a line from this point, the line with the highest slope originating from R_f touches the highest utility curve. A consumer wants access to the highest sloping line from the risk-free rate. In this picture, the gray line touches the gray curve: higher is better.

FIGURE **2.3.** *Tobin's separation theorem*

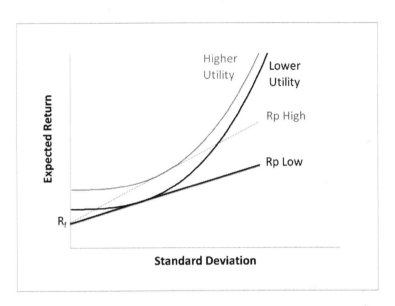

R_f: the risk-free rate (e.g., US Treasury Bills)

All the infinite combinations of volatility and expected return on a line connecting the risk-free asset's volatility and return, and R_p, the maximal Sharpe portfolio's volatility and return, are feasible given varying combinations of the two assets, R_p and R_f. A higher expected return/standard deviation asset, such as "R_p High" in the chart above, allows one to reach a higher level of utility because it creates a line, and thus a feasible set of portfolios, that touches the highest utility curve. This is the same as maximizing the Sharpe ratio, which is simply the expected return minus the risk-free rate divided by the portfolio volatility. What this means is, find the highest Sharpe for a portfolio containing only risky assets. The highest Sharpe portfolio allows one to reach the highest level of utility, regardless of the shape of your utility curve (that is, your particular risk tolerance, a).[28]

This is called a separation theorem because regardless of one's risk preference (one's a), the problem is separated into two independent problems: finding the risky portfolio with the highest $\dfrac{E(x) - R_f}{Stdev(x)}$ and then finding the point along the line between that and the risk-free asset that maximizes one's utility.

FIGURE 2.4. *Everyone holds the market portfolio*

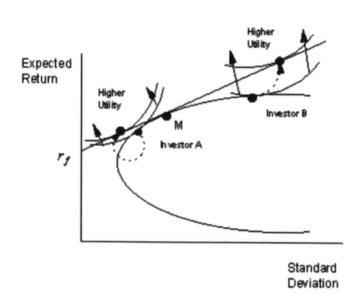

2.4 The Capital Asset Pricing Model (CAPM)

With 1,000 assets, you needed to calculate 550,000 different covariances to solve the Markowitzian problem and find the optimal tangency portfolio. In the days before modern computers, this was fanciful, but given Tobin's Separation Theorem, the problem for an investor turns out to be trivial. That is, if everyone is choosing the same risky portfolio to maximize their utility, then if supply equals demand, that portfolio must be the market portfolio. Thus the market portfolio is "M" on the above graph, the point on the efficient frontier that maximizes *everyone's* utility.

Four researchers independently derived the CAPM as an implication of Markowitz and Tobin's research, as Lintner, Mossin, Sharpe, and Treynor each showed that instead of looking at all the covariance terms, you could just look at the asset's correlation with the aggregate market.[29] Given the simplicity of the proof it is not surprising everyone was figuring it out around the same time, logical deductions being something organized science is very good at. The basic idea is that the market portfolio is on the tangency point of the efficient frontier. A few lines of algebra lead directly to the security market line, which is the capital asset pricing model (you can see a proof in endnote 30 below).[30]

$$E(R_i) = R_f + \beta_i \left(E(R_m) - R_f \right) \qquad (2.2)$$

Where β_i is the ratio of the covariance of asset i with the market, divided by the variance of the market (i.e., $\frac{\sigma_{im}}{\sigma_m^2}$).

This result is an emergent property of the seemingly innocuous assumptions mentioned, and not at all obvious, thus highly impressive—*if true*. This can also be derived by regressing a stock's returns on the market's stock returns.

We can measure the amount of risk via beta (β). What is the price of risk? The law of one price says that everything that costs the same has the same return, and vice versa. In this case, an asset's cost is a linear function of its beta because the beta is sufficient to tell us its marginal addition to the risk of our optimal risk portfolio, the market. Think of risk as a commodity, something that people must hold in equilibrium. It costs the same, per unit of risk, regardless of how it is distributed in the market via a single stock or a portfolio. The same beta must achieve the same return for this cost via a single asset or the market as a whole because otherwise one would buy the cheap one, sell the expensive one, and arbitrage the difference.

The security market line is the CAPM. Note the security market line is linear, in that beta is not squared or cubed. An exposure to priced risk will give you the same return regardless of how it's assembled: by individual stock, portfolio, or derivative. While the risk factor beta in the CAPM generates a linear return of $R_m - R_f$, the equity risk premium, and this idea generalizes to every other theory in asset pricing.

FIGURE 2.5. *The CAPM*

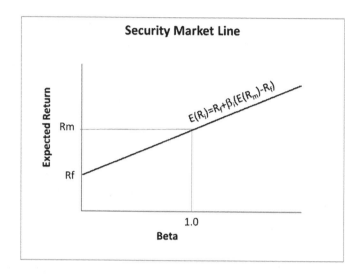

2.5 The Arbitrage Pricing Theory and Stochastic Discount Factors

The CAPM is a straightforward, testable theory. It predicts that beta is a sufficient predictor of returns, and the derivative of expected returns to beta should be the equity risk premium. All of these are observable, as betas are simply the ratio of the covariance of an asset with the stock market, divided by the variance of the market, which are also univariate ordinary least squares coefficients. The coefficients in a linear regression are often called "betas" in introductory econometrics, ergo the name, beta (as when a child names his cat "Kitty").

The most basic extension of the CAPM is the arbitrage pricing theory of Stephen Ross (1976).[31] The arbitrage pricing theory (APT) rationalizes throwing the kitchen sink against an asset's return because risk factors are constrained only by your ability to articulate an intuition for risk, which, considering the cleverness of top professors, is really no constraint at all. Even Fama (1991) called this framework a "fishing license" for factors.[32] Early APT models contained risk factors—the things you regress against a stock's return—such as inflation surprises, GDP innovations, shifts in the yield curve, the Baa-Aaa yield spread changes, oil price changes, currency changes, and changes in the slope of the yield curve. [33]

The APT is a simple extension of the logic applied in the CAPM, only to more than one factor using the "law of one price," or arbitrage. The idea was simple. Assume a risk factor has a price, as a beer does (e.g., $1 per beer). Then a six-pack must cost $6; otherwise, one could arbitrage this by either buying six-packs and breaking them apart or buying individual beers and aggregating them into six-packs. This holds for every factor relevant to an asset, creating a linear factor model in the risk factors, where the "how much" or "loading" is just a regression beta as in the CAPM.

Consider the standard Fama-French 3-factor model below, where we have a market, size, and value factor. Size and value factors are derived from the returns of portfolios of small, big, value, and growth portfolios, all designed to proxy these factors. The long-short portfolio mimics the underlying risk factors of size and value, though what actual risk they represent is hotly debated. Yet because they appear to have positive expected returns, it is presumed they must reflect some kind of risk. To estimate the expected return on a stock, you simply regress these variables on a stock's return using monthly data and then get the betas. You then apply these factor loadings to the risk premium reflected by the expected (aka average) values of the risk factors and generate your expected return.

$$E\left(R_i\right) = R_f + \beta_{i.m}\left(R_m - R_f\right) + \beta_{i.size}\left(R_{small} - R_{big}\right) + \beta_{i.value}\left(R_{value} - R_{growth}\right) \qquad (2.3)$$

The closely related stochastic discount factor (SDF) approach is based on work by Nobel Prize winners Kenneth Arrow and Gerard Debreu, who invented the concept of a state-space security.[34] These theoretical constructs would pay off a dollar if the state was on, zero otherwise, which generated interesting mathematics and was obviously general enough to cover all sorts of hypotheticals. Such "state contingent" thinking forms the basis of the SDF.

In the 1970s, the paradigm developed a momentum of its own, and economists proved many mathematical properties that would be nice for the discount factors to have. To get a flavor of this research, there was much rejoicing when it was proved theoretically the factors had to be nonnegative, meaning you would never get paid to receive a dollar in some arbitrary future state, as if this needed proving.[35] Rubinstein (1974) outlined the assumptions needed to reify a single consumer as a representative agent of the entire economy, and once he outlined the assumptions, the use of a representative agent was assumed with reference to this work.[36] These assumptions were insanely strong (for example, that everyone has the same beliefs about probabilities), yet most people did not think this was important because most economic assumptions are not technically true. Once identified, researchers often then take assumptions for granted as long as they give them answers they like, such as answers that are clever and potentially useful (circularly relying on the truth of the assumption).

General equilibrium models of asset pricing get down to stochastic discount factors, which is really a different way to generate the same form as the APT, which is itself just the CAPM with more factors. Enthusiasts see this as the alpha and omega of finance, a unified field theory of derivatives, yield curves, and equities because it generalizes to macroeconomic models of output and growth. The elegance and profundity of the SDF is essential in understanding the deep roots to the current paradigm in the face of its empirical failures.

The SDF approach is often called an intertemporal general equilibrium model because it can model both the real processes in technology and the preferences of agents in a representative agent model. This work starts with Merton (1971) and is expanded by Robert E. Lucas (1978) and finally Cox, Ingersoll, and Ross (1985). It generates the basic implication that returns of assets are a function of some risk-free rate plus a risk premium that is a function of the covariance of the return of that asset with the "marginal utility of wealth." Things with high payoffs when the marginal utility of wealth is high have high payoffs when the level of wealth is low (because marginal utility declines with wealth). The marginal utility of wealth can be proxied by a variable representing the state of something that affects utility such as GDP, the S&P 500, or consumption. As this state changes over time—due to recessions, changes in optimism about the future—it makes it stochastic or conditional upon current events. As this affects the risk premium, it is thus a "stochastic discount factor." Applying this to payoffs in states of nature, such as when things are going well, is a contingent-claims approach, and this seems insanely general because your contingency can be anything you can think of. The generality of the SDF is why theorists like it best. This approach leads to the CAPM as a *special case*, that is, back to

$$E(R_i) = R_f + \beta_i \left(E(R_m) - R_f \right) \tag{2.4}$$

(see endnote for a derivation).[37]

When a popular model is the special case of a more general model, scientists are especially impressed, as this reflects the kind of profound progress they aspire to, in that it is *like* a lot of really neat results in physics and mathematics. The SDF approach is based on utility functions and exogenous stochastic properties, which seems more fundamental than the APT, which is merely founded upon arbitrage. Most important, both contain and thus are consistent with the original CAPM. Researchers are relieved that they have not contradicted their mentors but rather merely extended their work, and everyone is happy.

The stochastic discount factor approach suggests we look for things that are proxies for wealth, broadly defined. Such things include the stock market but also inflation, exchange rates, wage rates, consumption, and oil prices. Whatever affects people's wealth is a potential factor. A security that pays off when times are good is not as valuable as one that pays off when times are bad, as one amplifies our wealth swings and the other dampens them, and we fundamentally do not like volatility in our wealth. The covariance of the payout matters, though instead of tying it to the market, as in the CAPM, we now tie it to the abstruse idea of one's marginal utility tomorrow.

The bottom line is that expected return is a linear function of risk, where you have risk factors that have positive risk premiums and risk factor loadings (or betas) that measure how much risk is being taken. The basic idea of the CAPM is that asset prices should be higher (lower) to the extent their payoffs are negatively (positively) correlated with the market, and this relationship should imply a linear relation between the covariances and the returns via arbitrage. No one thinks the CAPM works anymore, but it is still taught because it is so similar in spirit to the ultimate equation, an unimportant tweak that an MBA can fill in later (e.g., replacing the market return with the wealth/consumption ratio).[38] The theory integrates econometrics and utility theory, the basic economic toolbox. The pricing equations come out of several different derivations, and the assumptions seem innocuous enough.

CHAPTER 3

The Rise and Fall of Standard Models

3.1 Early Tests of the CAPM

The CAPM did not solve a paradox and did not integrate two previously dispa-rate theories; rather, it predicted something new—that returns were related to beta and only beta, positively and linearly, through the formula:

$$E(R_i) = R_f + \beta_i \left(E(R_m) - R_f \right) \tag{3.1}$$

The first tests of the CAPM were on mutual funds, partially because they attempted to show that good mutual fund performance was a function of beta, not managerial expertise. Consider the delight had by some academic prov-ing fund managers were irrelevant to their funds other than in what beta they incidentally determined for their portfolios. Another reason mutual funds were used was because as they were diversified the effect of beta on returns should have been clearer. Thus in the mid-1960s, the initial tests looked at mutual funds but basically did not find anything very compelling.[39] In spite of an absence of evidence, there was little concern this was evidence of absence—no "Beta Is Dead" articles would appear for twenty-five years. Often in intellectual history there is a presumption that if a bunch of smart people apply themselves to a problem with an existing theory that seems promising, it is only a matter of time before an almost solved problem will be solved. That the initial tests of the CAPM were not very supportive was presumably just a data problem, though with hindsight and the now rejection of simple one-factor models, they were doomed. When scientists anticipate empirical confirmation just around the corner, as they did in 1970, they are really much further than they realize.

The first most important empirical test of the CAPM was by George Douglas in 1969.[40] His approach was relatively simple, as all empirical research was prior to 1980. He took the monthly returns for 500 stocks over five years and generated a set of average returns, betas, and residual variances (residual being just the total variance minus the beta squared times the market variance). His results contradicted the CAPM, finding that only residual variance was significantly and positively correlated with returns. Lintner, one of the CAPM's discoverers, also examined the data this way and found that residual variance and beta were both relevant in explaining cross-sectional returns. [41] The seminal confirmations of the CAPM were provided by two works, Black, Jensen, and Scholes (1972) and Fama and MacBeth (1973). Their work employed a similar technique that seemed reasonable but inadvertently biased the tests toward accepting the CAPM.[42] Unlike Douglas, who took beta estimates as given, these approaches used a two-pass methodology to first form portfolios based on estimated betas then generate betas on portfolios grouped by those betas. This would reduce the "errors in variables" problem that occurs when high-beta stocks tend to be overestimated, low-beta stocks underestimated. That is, if betas are normally distributed with a mean of 1.0 and measured betas are simply the true betas plus error, the highest measured betas will on average have positive errors. So a stock with a measured beta of 2 on average has a true beta significantly lower, say 1.5, and a 0.7 estimated beta would probably be closer to 1, perhaps 0.8.

For both studies, the takeaway was that the security market line was positive as predicted—higher beta, higher return—and that was all everyone interested needed to know. Yet the slope was flatter than expected, and the results were not very strong, in that the slope was not significantly positive for any subsample, merely for the entire period from 1935–1968. These initial tepid tests were not corroborated, rather they remained the primary evidence of the CAPM over the next two decades.

FIGURE 3.1. *Returns and betas from Black, Jensen, and Scholes (1972)*

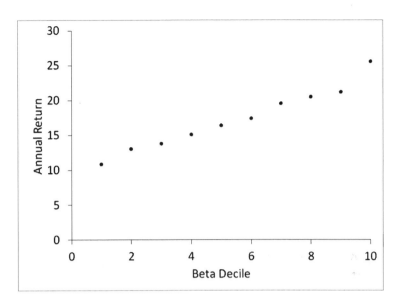

With the benefit of hindsight, we can see the bias in these works. Both beta and residual variance are positively correlated with size, a stock characteristic subsequently found highly correlated with returns. Both Black, Jensen, and Scholes (1972) and Fama and MacBeth (1973) created portfolios based on initial sorts by beta so that the resulting spread in portfolio betas would be maximized. This then makes the size effect show up in the betas because sorting by beta is, in effect, sorting by size. If they would have presorted by residual variance, which is also correlated with size, the results would have been the same as found for beta, only with residual variance as the explainer of returns. Presorting by betas made the spread in betas large relative to the residual variance spread and thus made the small-cap effect to speak through beta, not residual variance.

Of course, that is before all the work in the 1980s showing the size effect and how to correct for various biases that exaggerated the size effect. Nonetheless, it was somewhat inevitable that a theory touted as *The Next Big Thing* before any empirical confirmation was tested and corrected until the right answer was generated. Then everyone stopped making corrections and cited the articles prominently for the next twenty years. As we subsequently learned, there were many more corrections to make (for example, most of the size effect was measurement error), but with the right results, there was little demand for such scrutiny. In general, we test results with reasonable thoroughness, where reasonable is influenced by the plausibility of our result.

Around 1980, Merrill Lynch printed large beta books showing the beta for every stock. In 1990, William Sharpe and Harry Markowitz won the Nobel Prize for their work in developing Modern Portfolio Theory, which the Nobel committee considered to be the "backbone of modern price theory for financial markets."[43]

3.2 Later Tests of the CAPM

When the CAPM was being created, computers were very limited, so algorithms needed to be simple. Many empirical studies from those days look rather naïve, but one should remember the constraints they were under. In the 1980s, such constraints receded, and researchers left closed-form statistics such as ordinary least square or discriminant analysis and started embracing maximum likelihood functions that used iterative hill-climbing algorithms. A maximum likelihood approach avoided several technical problems in Black, Jensen, and Scholes and Fama and Macbeth by simultaneously estimating betas, intercepts, and slopes. Shanken (1985), Gibbons (1982), and Gibbons, Ross, and Shanken (1989) rectified several technical issues in the earlier work, testing the heart of the CAPM by whether the market is mean-variance efficient (as implied by Tobin and Sharpe). They applied Wald, maximum likelihood, and Lagrange multiplier tests, which have distinctions of interest only to economists and are a staple of graduate school exams.[44] Although Shanken and Gibbons rejected the CAPM at the 0.1 percent level, no one really cared about the substance of their results because given any sufficiently powerful test, all theories are wrong. Powerful tests on whether the CAPM was true were publishable, but everyone knew it was an almost impossibly stern standard. Such findings were published in the top journals and defined academic best practices.

Around 1980, the two most important counterfactuals to the CAPM were discovered: the size and value anomalies. Small-cap (that is, low market capitalization) stocks had higher returns than large stocks had, and value stock outperformed their opposite. Black, Jensen, and Scholes reported about a 12 percent annualized difference between the highest and lowest beta stocks, whereas size generated return differences of 15 percent to 24 percent.[45] Betas were larger for small-cap stocks, but this was insufficient to explain this big return differential. Within a year of the finding of the size effect, there was a special edition of the *Journal of Financial Economics* on this issue.[46] It turned out that much of the initial estimates of the size effect were simply measurement issues, and this is usually the case for such anomalies. A small-cap stock often has a low price and will often have a bid-ask spread, where market makers are willing to buy it for $2 and sell it for $2.5. If it closes randomly at its bid and ask, going from 2, 2.5, 2, 2.5, the returns are thus +25 percent, -20 percent, +25 percent, and -20 percent for an average daily return of 2.5 percent, which annualizes to 630 percent (252 trading days times 2.5 percent). In reality, its return is zero, which you would get by taking the geometric average or using log returns. This is a simple and pervasive bias in finance, that high frequencies returns are not indicative of real returns because they presume impractically costly turnover to achieve the arithmetic returns from constantly rebalancing one's portfolio. Blume and Stambaugh (1983) found this bias cut the initial estimates of the size effect in half.

Another large measurement error comes from delisted stocks that often have returns omitted the month they delist, which is rather convenient because the returns these months are particularly devastating—down 55 percent on average.[47] As small stocks delist much more frequently than large stocks do, this bias overstated the return on small stock portfolios. The effect was almost 50 percent of the size premium. The current estimate of the size effect is now around 3 percent.

Many investment portfolios now make distinctions for size (micro cap, small cap, and large cap). But the return premium for the smallest cap group is an order of magnitude lower than what was originally discovered around 1980. The key question today is whether this factor is a true risk factor or whether it's a return premium to characteristics reflecting behavioral biases (e.g., over extrapolating recent bad news explaining the value effect).

In contrast, the value effect is considered stronger than the size effect, though its discovery was much less auspicious. Initial estimates by Basu (1977) showed that the low price-to-earnings (aka P/E) stocks outperformed the highest quintile P/E stocks by 6 percent annually, which is much closer to the current estimate of what the value premium has been subsequent to its discovery.

This value effect shows up in many correlated metrics, such as book-to-market ratios or the dividend yield (see Stattman [1980] or Bhandari [1988]). These are all highly correlated ratios that relate a market price to some measure of fundamental value, such as book value or earnings. For some reason, the beaten down stocks, those whose stocks imply a weak earnings projection, tend to outperform. Unlike the size effect, however, this effect was not concentrated in January, and these firms tend to have lower-than-average betas.

In 1983, Bill Schwert wrote, "I believe that the 'size effect' will join the 'weekend effect' ... as an empirical anomaly," which just highlights that reigning anomalies change every decade, highlighting the confusing nature of popular anomalies. The weekend effect was part of the collection of seasonal anomalies very prominent in the early 1980s: the September effect (the worst month of the year), the January effect (small stocks outperform large stocks), the Monday effect (worst day of the week), the Friday effect (best day of the week), and the holiday effect (days before holidays tend to be good). For a while, the most conspicuous autocorrelation was mean reversion over three-year intervals (Werner DeBondt and Richard Thaler [1985, 1987]), though this later became overshadowed by its opposite, momentum (Jegadeesh and Titman [1992]).

CAPM pioneer Bill Sharpe remarked, "I have concluded that I may never see an empirical result that will convince me that it disconfirms any theory," which reiterated Fischer Black's (1993) feeling, "I find theory to be far more powerful than data."[48] These are not cavalier prejudices but rather the result of experience. The weekend effect, like the other seasonal anomalies, has disappeared. So like the latest miracle diet, the latest anomaly is treated skeptically by your average expert for good reason—because most have been dead ends based on selection biases or bad data.

3.3 APT Tests

In 1977, Richard Roll wrote an influential critique of the CAPM, noting that it was actually a tautology—that is, *if* the market was mean variance efficient (on the efficient frontier) and if people were mean-variance utility maximizers, then the CAPM's security market line held and vice versa.[49] Given that tautologies are not interesting, that implied to him the real scientific question is whether the market portfolio was on the efficient frontier. Given that our wealth consists of real estate, human capital, and many other things, any stock market index is surely not exactly the same. Given it is not exactly the same, the CAPM is empirically meaningless.

The Roll critique was constantly invoked to motivate the APT, in that because the CAPM necessitated the market return—and we can't measure 'the' market—well, an APT approach would solve this problem. When the CAPM was being sullied in the 1990s, Roll and Ross (1994) and Kandel and Stambaugh (1996) resurrected this argument and addressed the issue of to what degree an inefficient portfolio can generate a zero beta-return correlation, which by then was accepted as fact. That is, is it possible that S&P500 beta is uncorrelated with returns, though the true market beta works perfectly? In Roll and Ross's words, if you mismeasure the expected return of the market index by only 0.22 percent (easily 10 percent of one standard deviation away), it could imply a zero correlation with the market return.

This sounds devastating to tests purporting to reject the CAPM, but to generate such a null result with an almost efficient index proxy, one needs many negative correlations among assets and lots of returns that are hundredfold the volatility of other assets. In other words, a very efficient, but not perfectly efficient, market proxy can make beta meaningless—but only in a fairy tale world where many stocks have one hundred times the volatility of other stocks and correlations are frequently negative. Average stock volatilities range from 10 percent to 300 percent, most between 20 percent and 60 percent annualized. Betas for firms (not ETFs), prospectively, as a practical matter are never negative. This implies their proof was irrelevant as a practical matter, and that this reason was ever considered valid highlights that elite minds are very good at ignoring subtle inconsistencies when convenient.[50]

Tests of the APT started in the '80s, most referencing both the Roll critique and Ross's arbitrage pricing theory as inspiration.[51] Initial tests of the APT by Chen, Roll, and Ross (1986) were promising, as all early empirical seems to be in finance. They augmented the CAPM with some obvious macroeconomic factors such as industrial production, the yield spread between low- and high-risk bonds, and unanticipated inflation. As one of the authors (Ross) was a creator of the APT, it should come as no surprise that their results were supportive, yet only a few factors seemed priced. A stock might be highly correlated with a factor such as the inflation, but on average, stocks with a greater loading on this factor did not generate higher returns; the risk premiums were usually zero. This is what we mean when we say some risks are not priced. A good example is industry risk, which clearly explains portfolio variance, though on average no industry seems to generate superior returns.

Even though the APT approach of Chen, Roll, and Ross was intuitive—you could understand the factors they were suggesting—a new approach was being forged that seemed more promising: The idea that risk factors were statistical constructs, called latent factors because they were not clearly identifiable (and thus latent within the data and our minds). These statistical constructs appealed to finance professors who are relatively adept with the matrix mathematics of eigenvectors and eigenvalues, a branch of mathematics that has proven quite practical in physics.

Indeed, given a mean-variance objective, the latent-factor approach actually makes the most sense. One could come up with intuitive factors such as the yield curve and industrial production, but often these are correlated and so redundant, and there are methods more powerful than mere intuition. Nonetheless, the real problem with the latent-factor approach was that first factor (the latent-factor approach generated a set of factors with decreasing power), which explains about 90 percent of the total factor variance, is almost perfectly correlated with the equal-weighted stock index.[52] CAPM theorists could rationalize using either the value or equal weighted stock index as proxies for the market, and in practice researchers tended to use either or both without much difference.[53] You can argue the value-weighted proxy is more like "the market" because it weights stocks by their actual dollar size, giving more weight to Exxon than some $50 million start-up. Yet although value weighting measures the traded market better, perhaps the equal-weighted market better reflects the many unlisted companies that make up the true market portfolio. In any case, if either worked consistently better, we could explain why this index was what the theory requires, and researchers would have stuck with one over the other. Neither works better in explaining returns, so it really doesn't matter. As 90 percent of the latent-factor approach is indistinguishable in power to the CAPM, and there isn't a big difference between the value- and equal-weighted indexes, it was improbable this approach was going to bear fruit.

But even if the latent-factor approach were empirically successful, it has another large problem. Most researchers assumed there were around three to five factors, all declining rapidly in statistical relevance. Whereas factor one looked a lot like the equal-weighted index, the other factors were not intuitive at all. They were not correlated with anything you can articulate. Furthermore, many stocks had negative loadings on these secondary factors, so whereas the loadings on the first factor, as in the CAPM, were almost all positive, these other strange factors, with no intuition, had 60 percent of stocks with positive loadings and 40 percent with negative loadings. You could not explain exactly what the factor was, but presumably the loading implied that often you were paying for its insurance-like properties even though no one had any intuition about what this provided insurance against. That is, those stocks with negative betas for factor two were generating a return discount due to some indescribable insurance. I find it implausible that any investors implicitly or explicitly considered insurance of these unidentifiable factors a compelling argument.

3.4 Fama and French (1992) Change the Debate

The debate changed dramatically when Fama and French published a seminal paper in 1992.[54] Though Fama is now considered a leading researcher, when I was in graduate school, my more technical professors considered Fama to be somewhat of a lightweight, good at turning a phrase ("efficient markets") but not at serious research, which then were extensions of Gibbons and Shanken and their statistical tests or using Lars Hansen's generalized method of moments to test theories.

Anyway, Fama and French simply cross-tabbed the data to show any seeming beta-return correlation was solely due to the size effect. That is, size and beta were correlated, but if you controlled for size, there was no beta effect, whereas if you controlled for beta, there still was a size effect. In the words of Fama and French (1992): "Our tests do not support the central production of the [CAPM], that average stock returns are positively related to beta." So twenty years after the initial confirmation of the CAPM, where Fama played a key role, now we had rejection:

FIGURE 3.2. *Returns to betas from Black, Jensen, and Scholes (1972) to Fama and French (1992)*

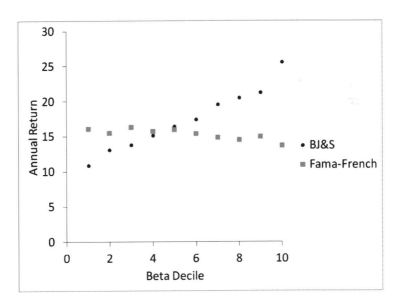

In the '80s, Shanken and Gibbons proved the CAPM wasn't perfect, which really was not that interesting because nothing is perfect. Fama and French showed it was not even useful. It's not insufficiently linear or insufficiently positive; its point estimate has the wrong sign! As with the boy's observation in Hans Christian Andersen's story "The Emperor's New Clothes," once Fama said it, everyone saw the CAPM's failure, as when in 1993 Stephen Ross noted as if it was conventional wisdom that in practice "the long-run average return on the stock, however, will not be higher or lower simply because it has a higher or lower beta."[55] The previous single measure of expected return was now acknowledged as not being useful, even as an incomplete measure of risk.

In Karl Popper's vision on how science works, theories produce falsifiable hypotheses, and when these hypotheses are falsified, the theory is then rejected and researchers move on. The CAPM predicted that beta was linearly and positively related to stock returns, and Fama and French showed this was clearly untrue. Yet it would be naïve to think that after letting such a fundamental theory take root for a generation, any simple fact would cause the academy to simply say 'oops!' Fama and French presented a "mend, don't end" approach to the CAPM. The paradigm would continue, just as the APT (or SDF) but now as a three-factor model, the now ubiquitous three-factor F-F model:

$$E(R_i) = R_f + \beta_{i,m}(R_m - R_f) + \beta_{i,size}(R_{small} - R_{big}) + \beta_{i,value}(R_{value} - R_{growth}) \qquad (3.2)$$

Note that this approach is really just the CAPM equation with two extra terms. The loading on the factor, $(R_{small} - R_{big})$, represents the sensitivity of an asset to this "size" factor, as measured by the beta on this factor from a regression. The final term, $(R_{value} - R_{growth})$, is the return on the high book to market (value companies) portfolio minus the return on the low book to market (growth companies).

Both the APT and SDF explain the addition of the value and size factors as risk factors because they are factors that explain a lot of cross-sectional volatility, and they are on average positive, suggesting they are priced and thus reflect some state variable that affects our utility. Working backward, because only above-average risk generates above-average returns, the anomalies imply some kind of risk. The APT does not care where these factors came from, but the SDF approach can give rigorous foundation to almost any factor one might discover. The result is a license to use whatever works, highlighting that the current paradigm does not so much illuminate as rationalize.

3.5 The Current Standard Model

Hopefully, more and better data generate stronger support for correct theories, as their truthiness tends to have more than one empirical implication. True theories get clearer as the data reveal them. Finance's new strategy to embrace old anomalies as risk factors easily misleads people to think progress has been relatively straightforward and cumulative.

The current standard asset pricing model is the three-factor Fama-French model with size, value, and the market. It has long been noted that size and value are not risks in any obvious sense, though over time researchers tend to forget this because the value and size effect seem persistent. Nonetheless, given value stocks have low betas, it is not clear how they are risky, and the high beta of small stocks would be a good explanation if only beta itself worked within equities. So in what way are small-cap and value stocks risky?

Fama and French first suggested that both the value premium and the small stock premium were some sort of distress factor—that is, they reflected highly improbable and nonlinear risk of a bankruptcy or some such catastrophic financial event. Intuitively, value stocks and small stocks had less access to capital markets and more risk of defaulting. It may not show up in correlations or covariances, but that's merely because such risks don't often show incremental symptoms, like how the first symptom of a heart attack is usually a heart attack.

Yet this initial explanation did not work for two reasons. First, it seems the characteristic of size and value, as opposed to their covariance loading, was their essence. That is, Daniel and Titman (1998) took all those small-cap or value stocks that had dissimilar covariances than their peers and found this did not explain their returns at all. The key attribute of a small-cap stock was not as the standard theory presumed, a covariance, but rather the size and value characteristics that were presumably mere proxies for something deeper.[56] They did this by simply looking at small-sized stocks with atypical covariances, and large-cap stocks with covariances much like your typical small-sized stock. Like most good statisticians, they just did some thoughtful grouping.

Daniel and Titman were agnostic on what size and value represented. It could be there were artifacts of historical data mining, accidental correlations one finds in any large sample. Alternatively, they could be symptoms of overreaction. Lakonishok, Shleifer, and Vishny (1994) argued the size and value effect captures systematic behavioral biases, such as our tendency to extrapolate recent data too much.

The other problem with the distress risk interpretation of the value and size risk factors is that when you measure distress directly, as opposed to merely inferring it from the size and value dimensions, such stocks deliver abnormally low returns, patently inconsistent with value and size effects as compensation for the risk of financial distress. Distress is a correlate of a high default rate, volatility, and beta, but also low equity returns.[57] Finally, there is the issue of what the market is doing in the Fama-French three-factor model if it does not explain returns at all. Here is the subtle attempt to not upset the paradigm that presumably underlies the whole approach. The idea is that the market factor is needed to explain the equity risk premium, the fact that equity indexes generate a higher return than bond indexes do. Thus the market factor, which Fama and French admitted is not relevant for distinguishing within equities, is necessary to distinguish *between* equities and bonds. One sees this a lot in the financial literature, as examinations of the currency or the yield curve use some parochial risk factors to explain some tendency within that asset class—but it is irrelevant to other assets.[58] Theoretically, any risk factor that works somewhere should work everywhere. Although in practice, this is never the case, and, as usual, no one really minds the inconsistency (e.g., if beta works between equities and bonds but not within, why would anyone hold high beta stocks as opposed to levering lower beta stock positions?).

In the end, we have a recursive solution in that return is a function of risk, which is represented by characteristics correlated with above-average returns. The longstanding anomalies of size and value were simply rebranded as risk proxy portfolios, which explain themselves rather neatly. The stylized fact of the equity risk premium, meanwhile, was always presumed significant and risky, though for some reason it does not apply to nonequities or between them just between equities and bonds.

There are always new anomalies waiting in line to become risk factors. For example, momentum, discovered by Jegadeesh and Titman (1993), is defined as a pattern whereby past winners over the last three to eighteen months tended to continue over the next three to eighteen months. Mark Carhart (1997) was the first to then add momentum (a long winners-short losers portfolio) to the three-factor Fama-French model and create a four-factor model in a study. Clearly, such models are descriptive in that if you can explain a fund's returns through momentum, this is useful. Whether it is a true risk factor is a separate issue.

3.6 Serial Changes to the APT

After Fama and French's 1992 paper, many people have tried to explain this result, but it is an embarrassment of riches. Reviewing the literature, there have been many potential solutions to the Fama-French set of size-value factors, but there is little staying power to the latest solution.

For example, Chen, Roll, and Ross (1986) asserted six factors as the (a) market return, (b) expected inflation, (c) actual inflation, (d) industrial production, (e) Baa-Aaa spread, and (f) yield curve innovations. Sharpe (1992) suggested a twelve-factor model, and Connor and Korajczyk (1993) argued there are one to six factors in US equity markets using principal components analysis. Jagannathan and Zhenyu Wang (1993) asserted human capital and the market portfolio are the two factors because a metric of human capital is needed to capture the total market; further, in 1996, they argued that time-varying betas can explain much of the failure in CAPM.[59] Lettau and Ludvigson (2000) used the consumption-wealth ratio in a vector autoregressive model to explain cross-sectional returns. Jacobs and Kevin Wang (2004) argued idiosyncratic consumption risk and aggregate consumption risk, and Jagannathan and Yong Wang (2007) cited year-over-year fourth-quarter consumption growth. All of these are perfectly consistent with general equilibrium approaches.

Although all this research is vibrant and ongoing, the diverse approaches suggest they have not begun to converge, even within the prolific Jagannathan/Wang community. The bottom line is that unlike value, momentum, or size, none of these solutions has generated interest in indexes because they are merely the result of torturing the data as opposed to any real pattern, which exists no matter who looks at the data.

The CAPM started with tepid confirmation though the seeming correlation between beta and returns was mainly due to the correlation with the size effect and this, in turn, was mainly due to measurement errors. Theoretical efforts in the 1970s and '80s focused on sophisticated statistical tests that got around technical issues, as with issues of endogeneity, but ultimately the simple empirical anomalies discovered at that time (size and value) highlighted the shortcomings of the CAPM. Size and value are now risk, and they do not explain other data, which makes sense for some reason we just have not yet figured out. Attempts to unify or generalize the model have failed repeatedly, yet the risk premium remains the centerpiece of finance, the idea that it is omnipresent and important.

CHAPTER 4

A Survey of Empirical Evidence

Existing theory is more of a framework than a theory, and frameworks are nonfalsifiable, every test merely of a particular theory the framework allows. The APT and general equilibrium SDF framework are healthy in academia because they can never be disproven, as any test of these theories is merely a test of one person's guess as to how to measure risk. Any single bit of evidence, such as the low return to highly volatile stocks, may merely suggest a new risk proxy.

Yet one can show such a framework is highly improbable by showing that the undiscovered true theory the framework allows must have some insanely improbable properties. Thus the most damning evidence is the scope of the volatility-return failure across many asset classes. I have never seen this evidence presented in a journal as an argument for the failure of the conventional theory, partly because such a diverse set of evidence does not lend itself to rigorous statistical analysis.

Whatever risk is, intuitively it should be correlated with the business cycle or the stock market or be volatile (or correlated with volatility). In practice, alternatives to 'the market' are either uncorrelated or positively correlated with the stock market. So if assets with high systematic volatility and covariances with the stock market are unrelated at best, and inversely related at worst, with average returns, it seems highly unlikely that a risk solution exists. That is, it defies credulity that the yet undiscovered priced risk factor is intuitively risky yet of low volatility with an inverse correlation to the stock market. Consider the following survey of asset pricing results and how they might fit with any potential risk solution.

4.1. Volatility and Cross-Sectional Equity Returns

My dissertation was based on the finding that high volatility stocks had slightly lower returns than average, and I argued this was related to the finding that mutual funds had a clear preference toward highly volatile stocks.[60] I documented a strong inverse relation between volatility and returns that was confounded by size and price, and so if you controlled for these characteristics, the pattern was really strong. That is why I started applying this idea in various ways and why I have been following the idea for almost two decades, and why I've written this book.

FIGURE 4.1. *Returns versus variance*

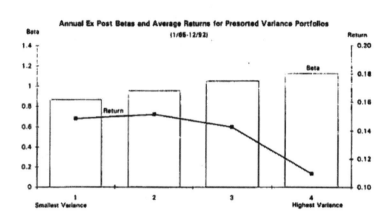

Source: *Eric Falkenstein dissertation, 1994, Northwestern*

I did a variety of analyses, and it was clear that volatility was anomalously and inversely correlated with future equity returns for most of the 1927–1992 period, and clearly had higher risk as measured by factor loadings or volatility. I thought this was dynamite, so much so that I did not care that professors were largely indifferent to my results because I thought it was going to make me rich rather quickly (see section 8.4 for my story).

Ten years later, several Columbia University professors—Ang, Hodrick, Xing, and Zhang—sought to estimate a new risk factor based on the beta with volatility innovations.[61] This is standard stochastic discount function asset pricing, looking for more subtle risk factors that could save the paradigm. What they found here was pretty boring, but incidentally they noted that the simple stock variance was negatively related to returns cross-sectionally. They followed this up with another paper documenting the result internationally (the initial volatility innovation forgotten, like most attempts to find risk factors inside the paradigm). This paper really is the first to make this finding—that high volatility stocks have relatively low returns—part of academic conventional wisdom, though many papers noted this incidentally previously.

FIGURE 4.2. *Cross-sectional annual returns for US equities sorted by total and idiosyncratic volatility*

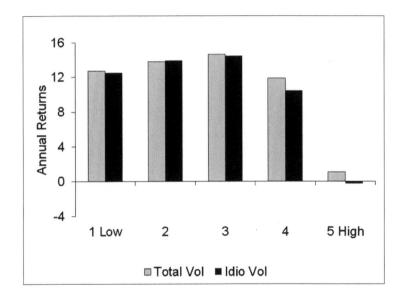

Source: *Ang, Hodrick, Xing, and Zhang (2006),*
Table 6. Returns are annualized from 1963 to 2000.

They found that stocks with higher volatility had significantly lower returns, and this held constant: book-to-market, leverage, liquidity, volume, turnover, and other variables, a pretty robust finding. The results above are for equities, and I think the essence of any real finding is that it shows up in a simple-to-read graph. You can see that the returns by volatility grouping are stable but then fall precipitously for the top quintile. Notice there is no real distinction between "total" and "idiosyncratic" volatility in terms of its effect on the raw-return spread. In the Ang et al. papers, they generated a residual volatility using the three Fama-French factors of the market, size, and value. In my dissertation, I also used both residual (aka idiosyncratic) and total volatility sorts, and these made no difference (in my research, I used the top five latent factors to generate idiosyncratic risk and applied this to the 1926–1990 sample).

Some have recently argued that the low-volatility effect comes from the value factor, and indeed low-volatility portfolios do appear a significant coefficient on the value factor that is comparable in magnitude to the lower coefficient on the market beta, and as the value and equity risk premiums are about the same magnitude, this explains the higher low-volatility returns.[62]

Yet this is unlikely because the effect is not symmetric. The high-beta stocks have negative value risk-factor loadings, about the same in magnitude to the positive risk-factor loadings on the low-beta stocks, but these high-beta stocks really suffer the greatest return fall-off. Further, the high-beta stocks have a much higher size loading, which should give them a higher return. Instead, for volatile stocks the return is much lower. Lastly, the size loading should lower the return to low-volatility portfolios, but that seems not to be the case. So if the coefficients on value, the market, and size are driving expected returns, the only part of that story that works here is the value/low-volatility connection; it does not work for the size/low-volatility connection, nor is it symmetric with the value/high-volatility returns.

TABLE 4.1. *Factor loadings for high- and low-beta stocks monthly data: 1964–2011*

	HML (Value)	SMB (Size)	Market
Beta-Low	0.29	0.33	0.58
Beta-0.5	0.42	0.15	0.61
Beta-1.0	0.25	0.28	1.02
Beta-1.5	-0.16	0.84	1.28
Beta-High	-0.36	0.97	1.61

Source: *SMB is the Fama-French size factor, HML is the Fama-French value factor. Factor data from Ken French. Author's data from beta portfolios available for download at www.betaarbitrage.com.*

4.2. Minimum-Variance Portfolios

Researchers have investigated minimum-variance funds since Haugen and Baker (1991), finding that a variance-minimization algorithm applied to a large set of stocks, including a no-short-sales constraint, generates about a 40 percent reduction in volatility compared to common indexes without diminishing returns. If traditional measures of risk are unrelated to returns, this is unsurprising and should be a straightforward way to create a portfolio with a Sharpe ratio that dominates the market. Curiously, all the papers that have examined minimizing index volatility also have found that not only can you create portfolios with much less variance than simple market indexes, but their returns were actually higher than the benchmarks.[63] In each case, the higher return was unremarked, instead emphasizing the lower volatility feasibility in a minimum-variance focus.

Minimum-variance portfolios are interesting in themselves because they are prominent in advanced textbooks on portfolio theory, as they form the leftmost point in the convex hull representing the set of feasible returns in risk-return space. Theoretically, they include long and short positions in stocks. The long-only approach of an MVP is attractive because many obvious stocks we all wish to short (for example, Palm in the 3M spin-off of 1999) in practice could not be shorted or have a large negative rebate (i.e., you get a negative interest rate on the short-sale proceeds). Rebate schedules and impossible-to-borrow lists are difficult to accurately re-create because these are over-the-counter markets. Furthermore, in many developed markets, one can short a minority of the stocks listed and proportionately less of the weak stocks everyone wishes to short. This makes long-short historical simulations difficult to interpret because one can never be certain it was feasible to implement.

Jagannathan and Ma (2003) showed that in constructing a global mini-mum-variance portfolio, a no-short-sales constraint actually helps out-of-sample performance because in an unconstrained approach, recommended shorts usually have very high covariances with other stocks. Stocks that have extremely high covariances with other stocks tend to receive negative portfolio weights, and the no-short-sales constraint is equivalent to capping the sample covariances at a reasonable level (alternatively, one can think of it as applying a Bayesian base rate to a covariance estimate that mitigates extreme correlations in a sample). Hence to the extent that high estimated covariances are more likely to be caused by upward-biased estimation error, imposing the nonnegativity constraint on position weights reduces the sampling error, and so a no-short-sales restriction is in practice a modest constraint in constructing a minimum-variance portfolio and makes the result something eminently feasible.

I constructed long-only, low-volatility portfolios MVPs (minimum-variance portfolios).[64] New index weights are calculated for each on January 1 and July 1 based on the prior year's daily returns using a minimum-variance minimization algorithm on the factors and factor loadings from Chris Jones's heteroskedasticity-consistent version of Connor and Korajczyk's principal components procedure.[65] Index weights are then constant for the next six months using a total return index, so there is no rebalancing bias due to equal-weighting daily returns of portfolio constituents. There is no survivorship bias because I use stocks that existed in the indexes at the beginning of the performance period; transaction costs are low, as these are highly liquid stocks and I am only going long; and liquidity issues should be minor because we are going only long stocks within the major equity indexes. Thus unlike the Fama-French size factor portfolio, with its many illiquid stocks and shorted securities, the January returns for the MVPs are actually slightly less than their sample average, suggesting there are no significant institutional issues due to end-of-year tax strategies that show up in illiquid securities.

Looking at the past fourteen years of data for the S&P 500, eleven years of data for the Nikkei and FTSE, and ten years for the MSCI-Euro Index, the table below shows that annualized volatility can be reduced by 30 percent to 45 percent within these indexes by simply reweighting the constituents in a way that minimizes the historical volatility but is then applied to the out-of-sample returns. Furthermore, in each case, the numerator of the Sharpe ratio was also significantly higher. The FTSE, Nikkei, S&P 500, and MSCI-Euro index would need annualized return increases of several percentage points to equalize the Sharpe ratios of their relevant MVPs. For example, the S&P 500 has an annualized geometric return of 3.6 percent over the past ten years, whereas the minimum-variance subset portfolio generated an 8.8 percent annualized return over that same period. As the volatility of the S&P is about 17 percent versus 12 percent for the MVP, in a Sharpe ratio perspective, the S&P return would have to be about 7 percent higher annually to generate a Sharpe equal to the MVP Sharpe. Betas of the MVPs range from 0.47 to 0.66. Thus as index funds dominate actively managed funds primarily because of their 1 percent cost advantage, the relevant advantage here is an order of magnitude higher.

TABLE 4.2. *MVP Statistics: 1998–2011*

	FTSE		MSCI-Eur		Nikkei		S&P500	
	Index	MVP	Index	MVP	Index	MVP	Index	MVP
AnnGeoRet	2.65%	7.48%	-0.62%	1.71%	-2.35%	-0.37%	3.63%	9.01%
AnnStDev	15.05%	12.10%	19.62%	13.23%	19.51%	13.20%	16.61%	12.43%
Beta		0.66		0.60		0.49		0.47
Sharpe	0.16	0.60	-0.23	-0.16	-0.26	-0.23	0.05	0.49
Start	Jan-01	Jan-01	Jan-02	Jan-02	Jan-01	Jan-01	Jul-62	Jul-62

Each index is formed at the end of June and December using a long-only subset of the corresponding index, where portfolio weights minimize the portfolio volatility over the prior year's daily returns. Beta is from regressing the daily returns of the MVP on its respective index. The Nikkei and Nikkei-MVP, FTSE, and FTSE-MVP use daily data from January 1, 2001, to December 31, 2011, and the SP500–MVP and S&P 500 use daily data from January 1, 1998, to December 31, 2011, and the MSCI-related indexes are from January 2, 2002, to December 31, 2011. The Sharpe ratio subtracts the average LIBOR rate for each currency from the annual return divided by the annualized volatility of returns.

If the most widely used equity indexes can be significantly dominated by simply applying the idea that risk is not rewarded using its very constituents, this suggests that the failure of the CAPM and its extensions is not a mere academic finding but something useful for regular investors. For those demanding concrete proof that their standard approach works in general, they should explain the minimum-variance portfolio anomalies because forming a portfolio based on the most conspicuous and earliest metrics of risk is not data mining the way book-market or momentum might be—this factor portfolio should sit at the top of one's list of things to test against a set of priced risk factors. As the returns to these low-variance portfolios are above the indexes, these portfolios should be most attractive to index investors.

4.3 Beta

Early tests of beta showed a slight positive relation primarily due to contamination from low-priced/small-cap stocks. These small stocks had biased returns from two sources. First, the bid-ask bounce for stocks that went from ¾ to 1 and back to ¾, showed up as returns of +33 percent, -25 percent, generating a bias from this unachievable arithmetic return. Secondly, up through the 1990s, such small stocks often excluded delisting returns, which Shumway found to be a significant -50 percent.[66] Fama and French famously cross-tabbed their data by size and found no relation between beta and average return. The result I document here is even stronger because I restrict myself to reasonably large stocks.

The table below shows the returns to various portfolios grouped by their betas. This used the investable universe, which was assumed to have a lower bound at the 20th percentile of the NYSE listed firms. As Nasdaq and AMEX firms are generally smaller, this gets rid of about half of the stocks actually listed, but it is more realistic in that it corresponds currently to about a $500MM market capitalization cutoff today. Most institutional investors are wary of going much below this because it gets difficult to put on large positions, and using the percentile we can account for the upward drift in the average market capitalization of this period—no ETFs, REITs, closed-end funds—all common stocks.

TABLE 4.3. *Total returns to portfolios sorted by betas: February 1962–December 2011*

	Beta-Low	Beta-0.5	Beta-1.0	Beta-1.5	Beta-High	S&P500
ArithMean	11.5%	11.8%	13.0%	12.7%	12.3%	10.7%
GeoMean	11.1%	11.7%	12.1%	9.7%	6.5%	10.0%
AnnStDev	13.1%	11.7%	17.5%	26.2%	34.4%	15.1%
Beta	0.58	0.57	1.04	1.44	1.82	1.00
Sharpe	0.44	0.54	0.39	0.16	0.03	0.30

Source: *Author's data from beta portfolios available for download at www.betaarbitrage.com*

Monthly betas use the prior 36 to 60 months as available. Beta-Low and Beta-High are the extremum one hundred low- and high-beta stocks. Beta 0.5, 1.0, and 1.5 are from the 100 stocks nearest these numbers. Portfolios are formed every six months. Daily data are used for betas after December 2000 and combined with monthly data using a two-thirds weighting on the daily beta, one-third on the monthly beta.

Data were taken from 1962 through December 2011. Only monthly data were used prior to 2000, but subsequent to that this was combined with daily return data, so that the beta estimates are better in the more recent period.

FIGURE 4.3. *Total returns to beta strategies: July 1962–December 2011*

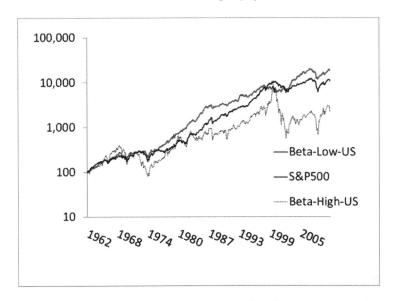

Source: *Author's data from beta portfolios available for download at www.betaarbitrage.com*

We see that average annual returns are highest for the Beta 1.0 stocks. Cumulative or geometric returns were clearly lowest for the highest beta portfolios, though the arithmetic average of monthly returns was much flatter. Sharpe ratios were highest for the low beta portfolios, and much worse for the high beta portfolios.

It should be noted that the cross-sectional beta finding is still held in some dispute. If you include all stocks, including low-priced stocks with substantial bid-ask return bias, the higher beta stocks generate inflated returns, and this generates a slight beta premium. As there are thousands of these stocks and they barely trade, I find this to be a simple mistake, the result of the rebalancing and survivorship bias.[67] Also if you focus on the monthly returns, and not the annual returns, you can get a slight positive slope if you choose certain subsamples. Nonetheless, researchers continue to try to fix the CAPM within the box, and many rely on there being a positive beta-expected return relation, if one that is weaker than expected; a negative beta-expected return relation really makes these attempts pointless.[68] Thus although I think the data are unambiguous, that high-beta stocks have lower-than-average returns, whether high-beta firms truly have lower returns than average is still disputed in some quarters.

4.4 Distress Risk

Early on in the size effect, researchers were at a loss to figure out what kind of risk that size captured, because beta was clearly not sufficient in explaining the effect. The obvious risk, residual risk from these very small stocks, was diversifiable and so not risk after all. Fama and French came upon the idea that both the value premium and the small-stock premium were related to some sort of distress factor—that is, value stocks, whose price was beaten down by pessimists and small stocks, which had less access to capital markets and probably had more risk of defaulting or going bust if the economy faltered. It may not show up in correlations or covariances, but that's merely because such risks are very rare.

Ilia Dichev had documented this back in 1998, but this finding could be brushed off because he presumably had a poor default model (he used the Altman model).[69] But then several others documented a similar result, and finally Campbell, Hilscher, and Szilagyi (2006) found the distress factor could hardly explain the size and book or market factors; in fact, it merely created another anomaly because the returns were significantly in the wrong direction. Distressed firms have much higher volatility, market betas, and loadings on value and small-cap risk factors than stocks with a low risk of failure have; furthermore, they have much worse performance in recessions. These patterns hold in all size quintiles but are particularly strong in smaller stocks. Distress was not a risk factor that generated a return premium, as suggested by theory, but rather a symptom of a high default rate, high bond and equity volatility, high bond and equity beta, and low equity return.

While I was at Moody's in 2000, I was able to use their database of ratings back to 1975 and found that the rate of return lined up almost perfectly with the rating, with AAA having the highest return, C the lowest. Updating that data using S&P ratings, I generated the following total return indexes by rating (delisted firms had their principal resubmitted to the portfolio after delisting). I use 1987 as the starting point in the table because prior to this, junk bonds (those with ratings below investment grade) were few, as there was a structural shift in the junk market in the late 1980s when these instruments started to have good pricing data (this does not change the results anyway).

FIGURE 4.4. *Total return to equities grouped by debt rating: June 1975–June 2011*

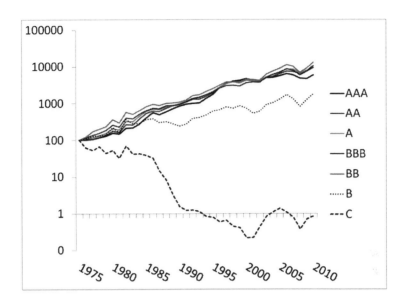

Source: *Author's data.*

Portfolios were formed every June. Firms delisting within the twelve months were then reallocated to the remainder of the portfolio.

TABLE 4.4. *Annual equity returns by agency rating, 1987-2011*

	AnnRet	Beta	Volatility
AAA	12.4%	0.78	17.1%
AA	13.9%	0.81	16.1%
A	14.3%	0.81	16.5%
BBB	14.2%	0.82	17.9%
BB	15.0%	1.04	23.4%
B	8.6%	1.43	32.0%
C	-12.7%	1.18	44.9%

Source: *Author's data.*

The returns are pretty flat until you get to the signature junk bonds, the Bs, and then it falls precipitously, and the Cs are even worse. Thus the equity returns to firms with low financial strength are lower than average using either a default model or agency rating. The initial hypothesis that value and size are really distress factors is, therefore, untenable.

4.5. Leverage and Returns

The Modigliani-Miller theorem states that regardless of the debt and equity proportions, the value of the firm is the same.[70] As a firm increases its leverage using more debt, its equity concentrates the variable returns of the business on a smaller and smaller equity base, making both equity and debt riskier; the equity's beta and volatility will increase, and the debt will have a higher chance of defaulting. Although total return is constant over a capital change, the equity and debt should both increase in expected return with an increase in leverage, as the lower debt return rises and becomes less of a weight in the total return calculation. The implication is that highly leveraged firms should have lower rated debt (junk) and more volatile equity, but because debt has a lower return than equity has, the total return to all a company's securities (debt and equity) is a constant.

FIGURE 4.5. *Annual return to portfolios sorted by market leverage (debt/market cap) adjusted for book/market and size exposure*

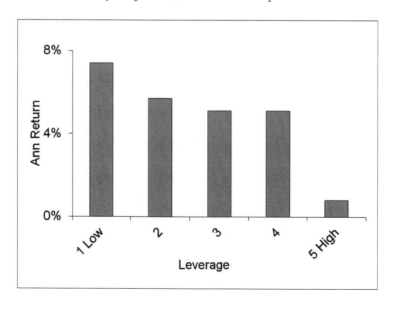

Source: *Penman, Richardson, and Tuna, 2007, Table 1*

In the figure above, we see that leverage is clearly negatively correlated with returns. These researchers held constant size and book/market, so that this leverage sort should not pick up these well-known anomalies. Higher leverage implies lower returns for equity, even though this should increase risk of that equity and thus should increase returns.[71] There have been no papers linking how leverage is positively related to expected equity returns, even though this result would have been consistent with a Nobel-prize winning theory. Empirically supporting Nobel-winning theory for the first time is worthy of a publication in a top journal, and for academics, this is their number one priority. The absence of a positive finding in this context is perhaps more powerful than anything else.

4.6 Penny Stocks

Penny stocks are a curious subset of equities, the ultimate small-cap subset, which are traded "over the counter." In the United States, the most active penny stocks are quoted on the Over-The-Counter Bulletin Board (OTCBB) and Pink Sheets. These two services collect and disseminate dealer quotations for several thousand of these stocks at any point in time.

Eraker and Ready's 2009 study highlights the abysmal returns to these highly illiquid assets. The average investor in the OTC market from January 2000 through November 2009 lost almost half of his investment. In other words, penny stocks are more like lottery tickets than small-cap stocks listed on the major exchanges.

TABLE **4.5**. *Annual return to penny stocks by volume and initial price filters: January 2000–November 2009*

Volume($)>	2,000		50,000		500,000	
Price>	0.01	0.1	0.01	0.1	0.01	0.1
Count	7372	6685	6423	5757	4603	3939
AnnReturn	-29.1%	-35.4%	-9.1%	-13.5%	-34.2%	-41.0%

Source: *Eraker and Ready (2009), Table 1*

4.7 Equity Options

Theoretically, beta—or any covariance with the elusive risk factor—measures the "how much" of risk. So if risk is priced call options with higher strike prices have higher betas, which implies a higher average return. Therefore, far out-of-the-money call options should offer extremely high expected returns as a percent of their price. As underlying non-ETF stocks always, in practice, have positive betas against "the market," all calls will have positive betas that exceed the beta of the underlying stock, and call betas will increase in the strike price as the calls get further out of the money. Hence all calls will have positive expected returns, and the expected returns will be larger for greater strike prices because the betas, as a function of the call price, increase as you go out of the money.

For example, say you have a stock with a price of 100 and buy a call with a strike price of 120, expiring in three months. If the stock price rises to 110 over the next month, the call option will rise about 120 percent, whereas a long stock position rises only 10 percent. This is the implicit leverage in an option—that is, it is like being able to borrow 10 times one's capital and invest in the market. It is exactly the same bet as an equity position, just higher powered. This is why greedy retail investors with inside information prefer options—you get the most bang for your buck in options if you know where stock prices are going.

Coval and Shumway (2001) proved that expected European call returns must be positive and increasing in the strike price, provided only that (1) investor utility functions are increasing and concave and (2) stock returns are positively correlated with aggregate wealth.

FIGURE 4.6. *Monthly reruns for call options ranked by their moneyness (strike / stock price)*

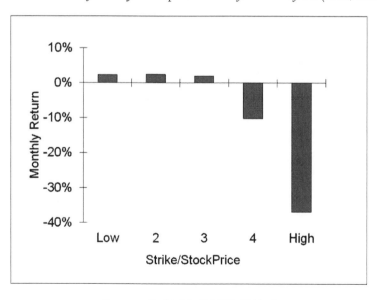

Source: *Sophie Ni (2007). Table 5*

Sophie Ni (2007) looked at data from 1996 through 2005 and found that the highest out-of-the-money calls, with one month to expiration, have average returns of −37 percent over a month. Figure 4.6 above shows that if you bucket call options into groups based on their "deltas," you find that call options, indeed, are highly leveraged stock positions. Lower deltas mean the call option is less sensitive in dollar terms to a stock moving but more sensitive in percentage terms.

Not only is the average return negative for call options, these returns get worse the more implicitly leveraged, the more risky the options become, in contrast to what is implied by the standard model. Returns are negatively correlated with the betas. Investors basically are overpaying for lottery tickets when they buy options, and just like the lottery, the average payout is worse the more risk one takes. If there's a risk premium in equities, it certainly is not amplified in options in any way because you lose money on average buying leverage market positions via call options.

4.8 Initial Public Offerings and Seasoned Equity Offerings (IPOs and SEOs)

An initial public offering has a great deal of uncertainty, especially for a quant wishing to apply a factor sensitivity to it, because there is no historical time series. One usually applies a factor based on its characteristics such as size, book/ market, and perhaps industry. Yet without a track record, these assignments are highly uncertain in the Keynesian/Knightian/Ellsbergian sense.[72] One would expect, given uncertainty aversion, these stocks to have positive returns to compensate for this risk.

Below are data from Jay Ritter, who updates IPO data and has been analyzing this for decades.[73] His main finding is that IPOs are horrible investments if you are not connected enough to be given a share at the IPO price. Getting an IPO allocation, as opposed to buying an IPO once it starts trading, is part of a quid pro quo with investment banks, where a desk buys "research" by paying a premium to execute trades and then gets to the top of the queue for IPO allocations, which on average rise 12 percent on their first day. Obviously, such easy money is completely internalized by the investment banker via the overpayment for trade execution. This is in addition to the 8 percent fee they charge to the issuing firm. Congressmen are quite adept at getting these allocations, and the SEC does not regulate how IPO shares are allocated.[74] Clearly, brokers find such IPO allocations useful for building relationships, but this is all a complex favor game, not a risk and return connection.

So the initial allocation is part of a complex web of favors between various parties. However, once on the open market (i.e., after the initial pop) where anyone can buy these stocks, the returns are below average, in spite of their much higher risk (see Table 4.6 below).

TABLE 4.6. *Percentage returns on IPOs: 1970–2009*
during the first two years after issuing

	Year 1	Year 2
IPO Firms	7.2%	7.1%
Benchmark	9.0%	12.7%
Difference	-1.9%	-5.7%
Count	8033	7914

Source: *Jay Ritter. See http://bear.warrington.ufl.edu/ritter/ipodata.htm.*

The effect also appears among the seasoned equity offerings. Standard theories explaining these findings tend to focus on the superior market timing of issuing firms, who seem to game the stupid, overoptimistic market. Some papers have argued that issuing firms merely have much lower risk due to their necessarily decreased leverage, and thus through the logic of Modigliani-Miller, a lower beta. But given the equity returns generate opposite results to what Modigliani-Miller implies among leveraged or high default probability companies, it would be rather odd if leverage and distress risk is priced only when the "leverage risk" is directly reduced via an IPO and not in these other tests.

4.9. Analyst Disagreement

Differences of opinion should proxy for parameter uncertainty, which is a qualitatively different measure of risk outlined by Knight, Keynes, and Ellsberg. Using analysts' earnings forecasts as a proxy for differences of opinion among investors, Karl Diether et al. (2002) found the quintile of stocks with the greatest opinion dispersion underperformed a portfolio of otherwise similar stocks.

Each month, they took stocks and sorted them into five groups based on size (market cap) and then within these groups sorted again into quintile based on analyst forecast dispersion, as measured by the ratio of the standard deviation of analyst current fiscal year annual earnings per share forecasts to the absolute value of the mean forecast. They found that the stocks with the higher dispersion in analysts' earnings forecasts earned significantly lower returns than otherwise similar stocks did. Specifically, the highest dispersion group had a 9 percent annual return deficit over the 1983–2000 period.

TABLE 4.7. *Mean monthly portfolio returns by size and dispersion in analysts' forecasts: 1983–2000*

		Size				
		Small	2	3	4	Large	Avg
Dispersion	Low	1.52%	1.45%	1.50%	1.51%	1.48%	1.49%
	2	1.12%	1.40%	1.41%	1.18%	1.35%	1.29%
	3	0.99%	1.20%	1.32%	1.11%	1.36%	1.20%
	4	0.76%	1.07%	1.18%	1.33%	1.33%	1.13%
	High	0.14%	0.56%	0.83%	1.03%	1.20%	0.75%
	Avg	0.91%	1.14%	1.25%	1.23%	1.34%	

Source: *Diether et al., 2002, Table II*

Diether et al. (2002) noted higher estimate dispersion is positively related to beta, volatility, and earnings variability, yet because the returns go the wrong way (lower return for higher volatility), they noted, "Our results clearly reject the notion that dispersion in forecasts can be viewed as a proxy of risk." Thus in spite of being correlated with all things intuitively risky the correlation with returns supposedly proves it is not correlated with risk because the one thing we know about risk is that it is positively correlated with returns. This is the kind of tortured inference you get when you believe in the risk premium.

4.10 Mutual Funds

The original tests of the CAPM were on mutual fund returns, in part because they would have lower idiosyncratic risk, which would presumably be easier to estimate both the expected return and beta. Thus in the mid-1960s, three of the CAPM creators—Sharpe, Lintner, and Treynor—published empirical papers on beta and mutual funds. Michael Jensen introduced the term "alpha" to the investment community by looking at mutual funds and attributing anything outside the CAPM model to the constant (i.e., alpha) of the regression. This early focus on mutual funds was forgotten once the early works of Fama and MacBeth (1973), Black, Jensen, and Scholes (1972), and Blume and Friend (1973), all found supporting data using individual stocks. Data that do not support the theory are simply ignored because they must be flawed.

As with leverage studies, the absence of any volatility or beta correlation with mutual fund returns is most relevant here because it highlights an absence of confirmation in an area examined since the very beginnings of asset-pricing theory. Absence of evidence is evidence of absence from a Bayesian perspective—not proof, but suggestive—especially when you know there has been a systematic, thoughtful search for such evidence. Carhart's 1997 study of mutual funds is most well known for introducing "momentum" as a factor, but, interestingly, a mutual fund's beta was never an issue in explaining the results. Risk is never found to explain mutual fund returns, so most papers have focused only on prior returns or prior alphas in the context of a Carhart four-factor model to explain returns.

Russ Wermers has the deepest history of looking at mutual funds, and in his *oeuvre*, there is a lot of adjusting for characteristics but not volatility, CAPM beta, or idiosyncratic risk.[75] Given the initial focus on mutual funds, its lack of subsequent focus for the CAPM highlights that there are no supporting data in this asset class.

Houge and Loughran (2006) found mutual funds with the highest loadings on the value factor reported no return premium over the 1975–2002 period, even though the value factor generated a 6.2 percent average annual return over the same period. Avramov and Wermers (2006) also reported little extra value via the standard risk factors. Risk in mutual funds remains something that was investigated at the outset of modern portfolio theory as a place to apply this theory, yet risk as a covariance has been found practically irrelevant in evaluating mutual fund returns.

4.11 Volatility over Time

The most basic risk models assume that the expected return on an asset is proportional to the expected nondiversifiable variance of the asset: the higher the variance, the higher the expected return. Modern models tend to focus on some abstract thing we don't like—such as declines in consumption, wealth, or output—but those bad states are generally coincidentally linked with higher volatility, as volatility increases when the economy is doing poorly. And so what do we see? Some research documents a null relationship between volatility and future returns; some finds a negative relationship; and some shows a positive relationship.[76] The results are ambiguous mainly because the pattern is so weak.

One problem with the data is that the model refers to expectations, and returns are actual events, not expected events. Volatility models may predict, but they too are only estimates of true expectations. Luckily, here we have the VIX data, which represent one measure of the market's expectation of stock market volatility over the next thirty-day period. The VIX is quoted in percentage points and translates roughly to the expected movement in the S&P 500 index over the next thirty-day period, which is then annualized. The VIX Index has been calculated by the CBOE since 1986 and began trading as a futures contract in 2004. If we look at the VIX levels and month-ahead S&P 500 returns as in Figure 4.7 below, we see no correlation. Prospective volatility does not predict aggregate stock returns.

FIGURE 4.7. *VIX level and future S&P 500 returns: January 1986–August 2011*

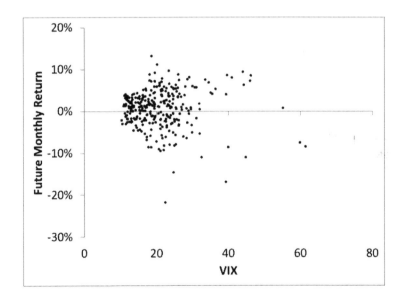

Source: *Author.*

Amromin and Sharpe (2005) used survey data and found investor expectations were totally inconsistent with standard models. They found that when investors have a more favorable assessment of market conditions, they tend to expect higher returns. Second, they found that the expectation of more favorable market conditions has a strong negative effect on expected stock market volatility. This finding is totally incompatible with standard models. Amromin and Sharpe's result really puts the standard model in a box. Unlike the CAPM betas, for which we can say we "just don't know the true market portfolio" (Roll critique), this result takes fewer assumptions, so its empirical failure is all the more fatal to the core financial theory. People should be increasing their expected returns in volatile markets, and on average that should manifest itself in actual returns. We don't see that in average returns using forward-looking volatility or in surveys of expected volatility and returns. A good signal of the importance of this result is that it has still not made it into a refereed journal for the standard objections referees find in such outside-the-box results.

An example of this finding is a Gallup Poll put out by Paine Webber.[77] In 1998, at the beginning of the stock market boom, they surveyed an expected return of 13 percent from investors. After back to back 20 percent+ returns when the Nasdaq doubled, investors raised their expectations to 18 percent in February of 2000, right before the peak. Two years later, after a 50 percent correction and a 50 percent rise in the VIX (a measure of expected volatilities), they anticipated only a 7 percent expected return. So from a Sharpe ratio perspective, when investors expect a high numerator, they expected a low denominator. They expect good times to be high returns and low risk and bad times to be low returns and high volatility.

Given the inverse correlation between returns and volatilities, where increases in stock prices correspond to decreases in implied volatilities and vice versa, this makes sense. That is, here in Figure 4.8 are the contemporaneous returns between VIX changes and SPX returns.

For buyers, this means they expect volatility to decrease as the price rises, as it does in practice (and is implicit in the volatility skew in equity options). Think of this as the classic physics thought experiment with Schrödinger's cat: a cat, along with a flask containing a poison and a radioactive source exist in a box. If an internal Geiger counter detects radiation, the flask is shattered, releasing the poison that kills the cat. The Copenhagen interpretation of quantum mechanics implies that, after a while, the cat is simultaneously alive and dead. Yet when we look in the box, we see the cat either alive or dead, not both. Similarly, in the future, the price will be up and the volatility down, or the price will be down and the volatility up. In theory, expectations should focus on the variance, which then implies an average return, but in practice, people focus on the return, which implies a variance.

FIGURE 4.8. *Contemporaneous SPX returns and VIX returns, 1987-2011*

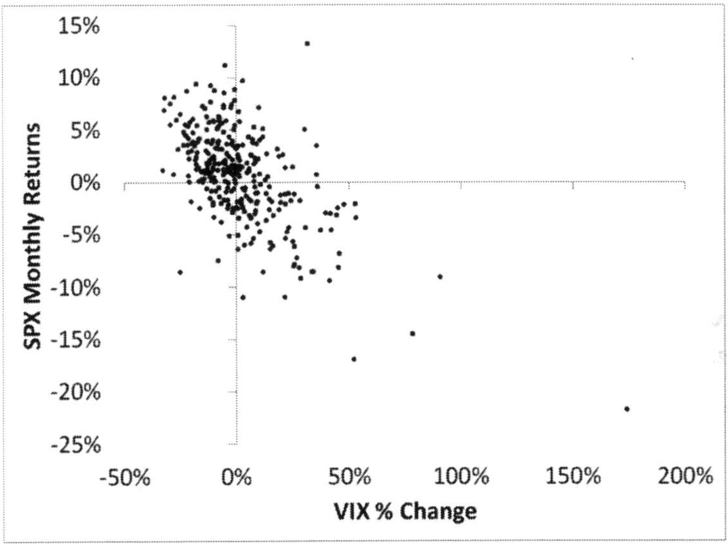

Source: *Author*

We do not have expectations based on standard risk models because if so, our expectation of higher returns would only be consistent with higher aggregate volatility. This implies most of our expectations are not based on a risk factor model. This is a bit like Warren Buffett's dictum that low risk means a high return because such pleasant scenarios had larger safety cushions to the eventualities.

4.12 Overnight versus Intraday Equity Returns

The returns from close to open dominate the returns from open to close. This is a paradox because close-to-open volatility is actually lower than intraday returns are. Below are returns from a total return index computed using overnight returns for the SPY ETF and the intraday total returns. One must use a traded contract, not an index, because index opening prints often include stale prices and, indeed, going back into the 1980s, you will see indexes with open prices exactly equal to their prior close. The ETFs, meanwhile, have actual opening trading prints.

FIGURE 4.9. *SPY total return to overnight versus daily returns*

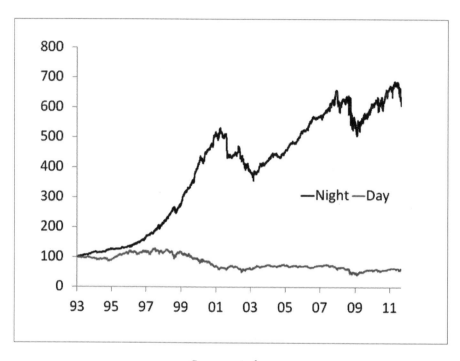

Source: *Author.*

The return difference was about a 13 percent annualized return differential. Given the arbitrage in this highly liquid ETF and its constituents, one can assume the average liquid stock also has this same overnight return premium. Cai and Qiu (2008) looked at twenty-nine different countries and found the overnight average return significantly higher than the intraday return in these countries, with lower volatility. Interestingly, they found this pattern was stronger in countries where short sales are either prohibited or relatively difficult. The result has been documented by others, though because it does not fit into any standard utility explanation, relegated to SSRN.[78] I looked at about nineteen hundred stocks using data from 2000 through September 2011, daily returns and excluded ETFs. I pulled this from Yahoo! and generated the following results:

TABLE 4.8. *Overnight versus intraday returns 1900 non-ETF US stocks: January 1, 2000–September 27, 2011*

	Day	Overnight
Beta	1.04	0.91
Volatility	3.00%	1.78%

Source: *Author*

So using either a CAPM beta or simple volatility, overnight is a less risky period than intraday, even though this is when all the return occurs. Both beta and volatility are lower overnight.

Another interesting data point is the behavior of the volatility intraday. I took about 650 of the highest volume stocks that were not ETFs. I generated a volatility metric by measuring the standard deviation of one-minute returns in the change in the midprice.[79] The data for each stock were normalized to 1.0 for each stock and each fifteen-minute period given average over those tickers.

FIGURE 4.10. *Average intraday volatility*

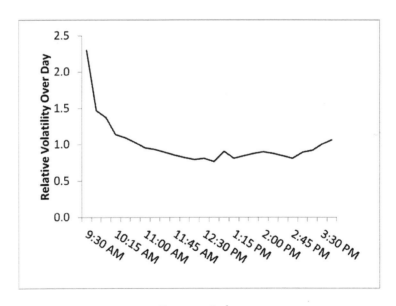

Source: *Author*

Volatility moves with the bid-ask spread, starting high and declining over the day, but it basically flatlines after midsession. A reasonable inference from this pattern is that risk in terms of volatility is much higher in the morning than at the end of the day. It also appears that adverse selection is probably greater in the morning, which is why so many market makers post such wide spreads (to avoid getting picked off by informed traders). Given that the biggest returns come from buying at the end of the session, not the beginning, the net intraday returns seem lousy by all accounts relative to the overnight returns, and difficult to reconcile with any risk story.

4.13 World Returns

Dimson, Marsh, and Staunton (2006) documented returns to stock markets over the incredible 1900 through 2005 time period—106 years. Using seventeen countries that represent about 90 percent of world market capitalization at the start of the twentieth century, they found an equity premium of about 3.5 percent, 2 percent less than the US return that dominates academic studies. Although this paper focused on average equity returns, an interesting fact in their data was the absence of any risk-return relationship *among* the seventeen countries. Looking at the standard deviation and returns, investors do not demand a higher risk premium in riskier countries.

FIGURE 4.11. *Average annual equity return premium and standard deviations in 17 developed countries: 1900–2005*

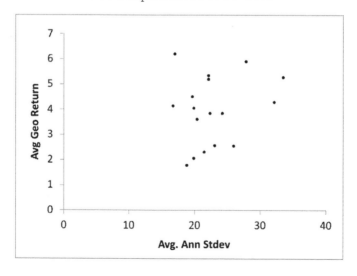

Source: *Dimson, Marsh, and Staunton, 2006, Table 3*

A look at emerging market stock returns shows the same pattern. Here are data from two separate studies, each with about twenty-five countries, from Argentina to Zimbabwe.

FIGURE 4.12. *Returns versus standard deviations for emerging countries*

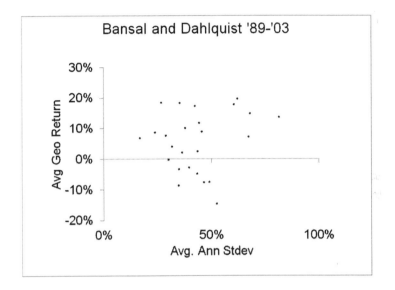

Source: *Bansal and Dalquist, 2002, Table 1*

In both cases, there is no correlation between the annualized geometric return and the standard deviation. Higher risk merely generates a higher volatility. The bottom line is that if you knew something about the relative volatility of various countries back in the day prior to any realistic ability to move capital into other countries, it would have been useless in trying to ascertain the future relative return of that country. Volatility *over a century* was irrelevant to cross-sectional returns, and this appears true across countries for both developed and emerging markets.

4.14 Equity Risk Premium

I do not dispute that equity indices have mean returns above risk-free bond returns in most countries. My claim here is that the equity risk premium most people analyze does not reflect the return to an average or marginal investor, merely the minority efficient one. Several issues create a wedge between the raw index return one sees in index time series and the returns flowing to average investors. Thus, a modest equity premium to the indices is consistent with my overall hypothesis.

The best single statistic that illustrates this subtle equilibrium is Ritter's finding that the cross-country correlation of real stock returns and per capita GDP growth over 1900–2002 is significantly negative.[80] That is, cross-sectional equity returns over a hundred years are not positively related to economic growth, so it is not as if the economy is a representative firm and a risk averse individual is choosing how much wealth to allocate to a stochastic investment; rather, the stock market is a subtle game between insiders and outsiders where the insiders merely provide enough top-line returns to keep the rabble unaware they are being had.

One of the most important constants in finance is the equity risk premium—that expected return on the signature risky asset, equities, over the risk-free alternative (usually long-term Treasuries). It is no coincidence that the CAPM's creation coincided with the creation of the Center for Research in Security Prices (CRSP). At the behest of Merrill Lynch, two professors at the University of Chicago, James H. Lorie and Lawrence Fisher, created what has become the preeminent database on stocks in the United States. In 1964, their database was complete, and they successfully demonstrated the capabilities of computers by analyzing total return—dividends received as well as changes in capital as a result of price changes—of all common stocks listed on the NYSE from January 30, 1926, through 1960.

The front page of the *New York Times* financial section heralded the pair's seminal article in the *Journal of Business* that reported the average of the rates of return on common stocks listed on the NYSE was 9 percent, about 5 percent above the comparable risk-free rate. Now, this was what actually was within a couple percent of the return on the Dow Jones Industrial average, a simple price-weighted index of thirty prominent stocks, but it was much more definitive, and as this was within only thirty-five years of the Great Depression it was rather startling to learn that stocks, which were considered incredibly risky investments, had over a long period a seemingly dominant return premium over bonds.

The result was extremely useful both to stockbrokers because it justified greater equity investment and to researchers because it was consistent with the new risk-begets-return theory of the CAPM. It was a bit like Dirac's theory, which posited there exists an antielectron via pure mathematics in 1928 and that was then documented in 1929. Rex Sinquefeld, now CEO of the quantitative equity management firm Dimensional Fund Advisors, noted, "If I had to rank events, I would say the original CRSP Master File is probably slightly more significant than the creation of the universe," which makes some sense if you think these data validated a new important paradigm.

The equity risk premium is one of the few risk premiums that is universally considered positive, too large even, which is a relief because in most areas the returns are decidedly negative for taking more risk. Mehra and Prescott (1985) famously introduced the equity-premium puzzle, stating that at 7 percent, it was too large for standard utility functions and their reasonable parameters. Most estimates today are around 3.5 percent annually for most academics publishing in this field and 5 percent for practitioners.[81] Considering that most economists see the long-run real GDP growth for the economy at about 3 percent, if equity returns are truly 2 percent higher than this in only fifty years GDP will equal dividends on the stock market—an absurdity.[82] Thus this important data point has *moved* about 3.5 percent from something logically impossible to its current level over the past twenty-five years, and suggests that the adjustment I am recommending (i.e., zero) is not without precedent, especially in the qualified way I am proposing.[83]

As mentioned in the introduction, the Investment Company Institute sponsored a study and found actual investors underperformed the S&P 500 for the ten-year period from December 31, 2000, through December 31, 2010, by 6 percent annually. Fund complexes and the Investment Company Institute were very loathe to present this information because it highlighted that they are severely over representing investor returns by using simple indexes, ignoring the many slips between cup and lip in the investment process. Luckily for the investing community, individual investors accommodate this misrepresentation, as even highly educated investors overestimate their personal returns by this order of magnitude (i.e., 6 percent annualized return).[84] This is probably due to simple cognitive dissonance, as investors are mentally distressed by the conflict between a good self-image and empirical evidence of poor trading tactics. To reduce the discomfort, investors adjust their memory about that evidence and those choices. This is then selectively reinforced by noticing the returns of just their good performing stocks and mutual funds in the portfolio and not the poor ones. The dramatic overestimation of typical individual returns via the benchmarks is a rather important, and unremarked, fact.

The actual net returns to average investors remain something of little interest to modern research. Note that prior to the competition from electronic trading, discount brokerages, the deregulation of commissions in 1975, and the reintroduction of odd-eighths quotes on the Nasdaq in the 1990s, trading costs were certainly much higher, yet most researchers look merely at the top line of the indexes as these costs were irrelevant, and top line pre-1975 returns are the same to investors as they are subsequently. If average investors are looking at their returns after fees and taxes, these costs should be highly relevant, but instead they are routinely ignored. This highlights a very strange incuriosity with net returns to investors.

Consider the following annualized adjustments that mainstream economists apply piecemeal, though when considered in total take the current estimate well below zero for your average investor:

Geometric versus Arithmetic Averaging:

If you think about equity investing as a plan to accumulate assets over 30 to 40 years, the cumulative geometric return is going to be less than the average annual returns. The adjustment to monthly returns is approximately the arithmetic return minus half the annualized variance divided by 2. If you keep a fixed investment amount at all times you earn the arithmetic average return, while if you invest an initial amount and never add or subtract, you earn the geometric average return. Which one is more relevant depends on how frequently you rebalance your investment. This issue is larger the larger the volatility of the investment in question. As the US equity volatility has been on average 20 percent, the variance is 4 percent divided by 2, and the adjustment is 2 percent. Dimson, Marsh, and Staunton (2006) actually looked at specific country indexes to arrive at this same adjustment number. Most but not all equity premium estimates adjust for this difference, which is a major change over the past 20 years.

Survivorship Bias/Peso Problems:

The United States was one of the best markets in the twentieth century so not a representative data point for an average going forward. Dimson, Marsh, and Staunton (2006) estimated that the survivorship bias of the United States should lower the expected premium across the world by 2 percent to about 3–3.5 percent. Czechoslovakia, Hungary, Poland, Russia, and China all experienced −100 percent returns, which are probably relevant data points for a forward-looking US equity premium but were excluded from Dimson et al.'s data. Authors of the peso problem literature pointed out that low-probability events, such as something that happens 2 percent of the time annually, are often not observed in sample.[85] Barro (2006) surveyed a number of financial collapses in the twentieth century and found that this adjustment suggested a 3 percent reduction to equity risk premia, emphasizing that if the United States could easily have had an experience like Argentina's, the world equity premium would be vastly lower.[86]

One should note that data from the nineteenth century, as presented by Jeremy Siegel in his book *Stocks for the Long Run*, are very suspect. Stock indexes from that period would typically contain a large amount of survivorship bias, as every couple of generations a professor would look at an industry that survived on the one exchange that flourished (Charleston, New Orleans, and Norfolk had vibrant exchanges in the United States at one time) and then take within that those stocks with complete data over a period. One should remember that in 1774, the colonial South had about twice the per capita income of New England, and their subsequent slow growth corresponded with the disappearance of their exchanges.[87] One should be very skeptical of top data points pre-1900.[88] Similarly, bond returns were vastly different in the nineteenth century, and back then bonds were relatively more important and default rates were several times larger for the entire market from 1870–1925. For example, Giesecke et al. found that the total default rate for the 1873–1875 period was a whopping 36 percent, which for an entire bond market is much larger than what occurred in the Great Depression.[89] This highlights that even a century is not a lot of data, and it is useful to contemplate other data that help inform one's sample data.

Taxes:

The original paper on the returns-to-equity investing by Lorie and Fisher back in 1964 found that those in the top tax bracket had a 2.2 percent lower annualized return than the top-line returns, applying the tax codes in operation from 1926–1960. Since this initial study, tax-adjusted returns have been basically ignored.

Investors care about their after-tax return, not pretax, and this is relevant because the tax rate will compress an equity premium. That is, consider a risk-free rate of 5 percent and an equity return of 11 percent. At a tax rate of 40 percent, the risk-free rate becomes 3 percent and the equity return 6.6 percent, reducing the equity premium from 6 percent to 3.6 percent. Given the multidimensional matrix of parameters changing over time, we can only estimate the average effect of taxes on the after-tax return. Jeremy Siegel differentiated between long-term and short-term gains and the differing tax rate on dividends.[90] He assumed a 5 percent average annual turnover, which is extremely conservative given that the average mutual fund has a 100 percent turnover. He calculated that from 1926 through 1997, taxes reduced the equity premium above US Treasury bonds from 5.2 percent to 4.0 percent for the top bracket and 4.7 percent for the lowest tax bracket, which is a reduction of 0.5 percent to 1.2 percent from the pretax equity premium. In a totally different study, Maymin and Fisher (2011) found that the average tax cost to mutual fund investors over the 1996–2010 period was 1.63 percent.

Niall Gannon and Michael Blum modeled the after-tax returns more meticulously.[91] They modeled a portfolio that began in 1961 and saw identical returns to the S&P 500 Index and assumed a 20 percent annual turnover, on which it paid long-term capital gains tax at the highest rate. The model portfolio also received annual dividends based on the dividend yield of the index on which it paid taxes at the highest rate. This generated a 6.72 percent annual return, a 5.28 percent reduction compared to the CRSP NYSE-AMEX market-weighted index as calculated by Kenneth French. During the same period studied, the Long-Term Municipal Bond Buyer Index had a straight-line average return of 6.14 percent with about one-third the volatility. That is, the equity premium was reduced to 58 basis points by taxes.

The interesting point here is that this assumed a 20 percent annual turnover. Odean and Barber (2000) found that the average individual retail investor turns over his portfolio 60 percent each year.[92] Furthermore, as most equity investors are undiversified, their volatility will be higher than the market's, leading to greater tax losses.

Adverse Market Timing:

In analyzing the returns of stock investors from 1950 to 2002, researchers typically refer to an average buy-and-hold return for some widely used stock index such as the Standard and Poor's 500. But consider a different measure of returns, one that weights time periods by how much money was at work. This is most relevant to funds that generate greate returns when there are incubating with paltry sums, then are sold and become really large, and their subsequent performance is poor. Should you just take a simple average of the annual returns, or weigh the later periods when they had 10 times as much capital at work relatively more? To the extent market inflows tend to crowd around market peaks, the average return experienced by investors will be less than if we equal weight the periods.

Share issuance changes come from seasoned equity offerings, stock buy-backs, issuing warrants, employee stock purchase plans, restricted grant shares to executives, and equity options to employees. A good anecdote is Evergreen Solar (ticker: ESLRQ), which bought a total of $446 million in shares from 1996–2010. Alas, most of this occurred at the peak of their price, allowing insiders to cash out during a period of excessive optimism, so the returns over ten years averaged a poor −10 percent, if one looked solely at the price, but a whopping −47 percent if one looked at the internalized rate of return from November 2000 through December 2010. They later went bankrupt, but the point remains: shares were issued strategically at highs, allowing insiders to benefit substantially, whereas outsiders who bought the shares were basically left with nothing.

Evergreen's case was not anomalous but rather part of a pattern. Stock inflows in aggregate, measured as new issuances of equity minus stock buy-backs, are positively correlated to recent stock returns—that is, people invest more new money into stocks after good times, not bad. An index may move from 100 to 200 to 100, and this return is zero if viewed at periodic returns, yet if one is investing equal share amounts each period—and thus correlated dollar amounts that are correlated with the returns—the return is actually negative. Dichev (2005) looked at a variety of indexes and equity net inflows and found this adjustment reduces returns by 1.3 percent for NYSE/AMEX for the period 1926–2002; 5.3 percent for the Nasdaq from 1973–2002; and 1.5 percent for nineteen major international stock exchanges from 1973– 2004.[93] Maymin and Fisher (2011) found that over a fifteen-year period through 2010, mutual fund investors underperformed their mutual fund investment class by 1.95 percent due to poor timing alone.

Transaction Costs:

When I started a fund in 1996 to demonstrate the value of low-volatility investing, I had little experience and no trading mentor. I sent a fax of share amounts for the various tickers. I remember my all-in costs the first day—commissions and crossing the spread just opening positions—was 2.0 percent, and I was trying much harder than your average investor to minimize this expense. I got this down, but this highlights how expensive it is to trade, especially when you are not experienced at finding the low-cost brokers and tactics.

Transaction costs include commissions, fees, spreads, and price impact. Although commissions and fees are straightforward, these are currently (2011) small relative to the spread and price impact. Indeed, brokers profit from commissions, spread, and market impact, so they often play "bait-and-switch" in marketing, akin to how razor manufacturers sell their razors below cost and make it up on the razor blades refills in the long run.

Historically, however, commissions were about 60 cents/share (about 1.5 percent) until the 1975 deregulation, and are currently about 2 cents a share (about 0.1 percent) on average. Plus, mutual funds often had 8.5 percent fees until the 1970s. Barber and Odean looked at discount brokerage data from the 1990s and estimated a sum of spread and commission to be about 2 percent of the price.[94] Jones estimated that the one-way commission rate on NYSE stocks was about 0.82 percent in 1962.[95]

Currently, institutions pay about 0.5 cent a share for VWAP trades that allocate a trade's impact across the entire day's trading (VWAP is the 'value weighted average price'). This price basically pays for the inevitable bid-ask spread one pays relative to an average price and includes the commission. If you assume that every year you rebalance that you need two trades (one to sell, another to buy), that is about a 0.1 percent cost for the sophisticated institutional investors. Yet this does not include the price impact, as VWAP trades ignore this effect—that is, if you push the average price upward via your trading, you have to pay for this. This effect is, in my experience, at least three times the explicit fee, something brokers are keen to ignore when selling their algorithms. Basically, you need to take the price prior to trading and compare it to the average price transacted but only for those trades you made that did not include a major price change signal so that buys and sell reflect just your execution pressure on average. This takes many trades and proprietary data, which is why it is ignored by academics. Just because this cost does not go to the broker does not mean it does not exist, and buying moves prices against you in the same way that measuring an electron changes its position.

Thus I would say annual costs are at least 0.5 percent for the most efficient traders and considerably worse for retail traders who simply cross the spread. More important, historically over the twentieth century, costs were considerably higher. An index fund may currently offer a near zero or even a negative in transaction costs (they benefit from market power when lending out shares for short sellers). Yet these are a small proportion of investors today, and for most of the twentieth century were not a meaningfully large proportion of capital invested in equities. For the average investor over the past eighty years, the sum of commission, bid-ask, and trade impact costs was easily around 2 percent annually.

Sum of Corrections:

The bottom line is these are all individually reasonable adjustments, each promoted in solid journal articles, claiming to half the equity risk premium. Their net effect, however, is to demolish the equity risk premium.

TABLE 4.8. *Equity premium adjustments*

Geometric vs. arithmetic averaging	2.0 percent
Survivorship bias/peso problems	2.0 percent
Taxes	2.0 percent
Adverse market timing	2.0 percent
Transaction costs	2.0 percent
Sum	10.0 percent

These are all conservative estimates to our 1900–2010 data, and they add up to an adjustment to the effective equity risk premium well below zero, using reasonable estimates for each of these issues. Most papers have addressed one of these issues and then note that such an issue (peso problem, taxes, etc.) can explain much of the equity premium. Note that the DALBAR study mentioned above estimates a 5.9 percent annualized deficiency relative to the equity index averages—ignoring taxes. Fortunately for brokers, individual investors have bad memories, as Goetzmann and Peles (1997) found that individuals overestimate their own investment performance by an average of 3.4 percent. In so many ways, investors are like gamblers, as with all those people who recall their last trip to Las Vegas left them flat or up a little.

The equity risk premium can be thought of as a subtle part of an equilibrium where the efficient investor who makes a 3% premium is the loss-leader and the average investor more than makes up for this 'expense' to the insiders. Though an efficient investor may be able to invest in efficient passive funds and capture much of the equity premium, such an investor is the exception in the same way that your average blackjack player loses considerably more per hand than when he is playing perfectly. That is, just as most hedge fund profits go to hedge fund owners, most outside equity investment goes to insiders—brokers, management, initial equity owners—via the persistent mistakes and carelessness of your average equity investor. Equity returns are not simply a stochastic process that a singular representative investor chooses, but rather a complex array of returns depending on the strategy and tactics used by heterogeneous investors, many of whom make conspicuously inefficient choices with statistical certainty. Your average equity investor probably makes less than a zero "risk premium."

4.15 Entrepreneurial Investments

Entrepreneurial investment, such as in small proprietorships (partnerships, proprietorships, S corps, C corps), are highly undiversified investments for most entrepreneurs. The reasons are straightforward in that when one person has a significant effect on the business through his effort and competence, it is natural that he should have the most skin in the game to align his incentives with the performance of the firm. This is a classic issue of moral hazard because a business manager who has significant upside but little downside would be motivated to take wild risks on the theory of heads I win, tails the banker loses.[96] However, if the manager is the majority owner, his failure would affect his net wealth too much for such recklessness.

In the United States, the richest 20 percent own 83 percent of the net worth and 95 percent of financial assets. The median rich household invests about half of its wealth in undiversified private equity, and about 75 percent of all private equity is owned by households for whom it constitutes at least half of their total net worth. Furthermore, households with entrepreneurial equity invest on average more than 70 percent of their private holdings in a single private company in which they have an active management interest. Despite this dramatic lack of diversification, private investment returns are on average no higher than the market return on all publicly traded equity. The chart below shows the basic results of Moskowitz and Vissing-Jorgensen (2002), that over an eight-year period, if anything returns to private business, there is no demonstrable premium.[97] Given an investor can invest in a diversified, liquid equity portfolio, it is puzzling why households willingly invest substantial amounts in an asset with an equivalent return but much higher volatility, including a positive correlation with the market.

FIGURE 4.13. *Annual returns to private investments: 1990–1998*

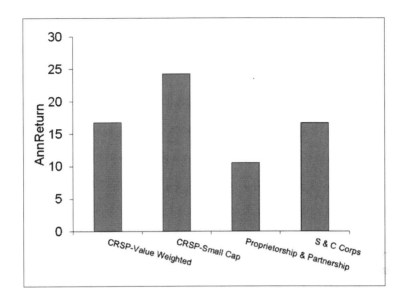

Source: *Moskowitz and Vissing-Jorgensen, 2002, Table 4.*

The forced nondiversification of a private equity investment from a pure portfolio perspective implies a requisite higher return. How much higher than the average public equity return would we expect the average private equity return to be? Using standard utility models to calibrate the hurdle rate that would make a household indifferent between investing in a single private firm or a public equity index, researchers estimate that private equity risk generates a hurdle rate of about 10 percent higher than the public equity return.[98] You should receive a huge premium for the large idiosyncratic risk you are taking, risk that unlike idiosyncratic risk in the market is impossible to diversify away. Although this is not a very long data set in terms of time, it is all the data we have, and it suggests that entrepreneurs appear to be taking a lot of extra risk for no extra return.

4.16 Private Equity

A related field is private equity, which is more arms-length equity investing than private-firm investing. The typical investment structure is a partnership where a private equity firm serves as the general partner and acts as the investment manager while external investors provide funding as limited partners. The best rewards come when such investments are turned into IPOs, in which the initial investors then reap large returns selling their shares to the general public. Such funds are less liquid and carry greater operational risk than a standard public equity index investment does. Harvard and Yale have two very successful, well-known private equity funds for managing their large endowments.

Cambridge Associates is an adviser to private equity investors and maintains an index of private equity performance, which as of March 2011 they noted has a 3 percent annual premium over the S&P 500.[99] For asset classes like private equity, data are difficult to come by and usually presented by firms with a clear interest in positively portraying the asset in question. For example, the Credit Suisse/Tremont Index that monitors hedge fund returns is maintained by the following:

> The joint venture, Credit Suisse Tremont Index LLC, combines the considerable expertise of Credit Suisse, one of the world's leading global investment banking firms, and the data research group of Tremont Capital Management, Inc., a full-service hedge fund of funds investment management firm.

Clearly, this provider wants the indexes to project favorable returns. Or consider art indexes, such as the Mei-Moses Art Index.[100] It generates an index based on matched sales: sales of the same piece over different dates are used to generate a return. This has a survivorship bias because pieces bought that were never sold again do not make the index, and such pieces are disproportionately those that have fallen in value. When art funds were actually created in 2007 (e.g., Carlson's Art Trading Fund), most were disbanded in 2009 after large losses from the recession and probably will be excluded from any art index returns going forward.

It is an inevitable conflict of interest when those most knowledgeable have access to the best data and are invariably interested advocates—after all, one does not become extensively knowledgeable in something one thinks is inefficient. Remember that it was conventional wisdom that active portfolio managers outperformed passive indexes until the 1970s—for several decades—because the evidence was generally held and presented by the active managers and their industry groups with various survivorship and other biases.

Kaplan-Schoar (2005) reported after-fee average returns for limited partners no better than the S&P 500 over the 1980–2001 period. Phalippou-Gottschalg

(2009) documented worse results after adjusting for selection biases related to voluntary reporting, which imparts a survivorship bias. Both Faber-Richardson (2009) and Ilmanen (2011) concluded the returns of private equity are at best equal to that for the broad stock market, probably a little lower.

4.17 Currencies

A currency is not just a medium of exchange, but an asset with a return, like a stock. The interest rate is like a dividend, the change in spot price, the capital appreciation. One would expect the return of currencies to be related to risk so that investors choosing to invest in yen, euros, or dollars are compensated for risk.

Uncovered interest rate parity is a theory that connects current to future spot rates. This theory states that you have two ways of investing, which should be equal. First, you can invest in your home country at the riskless rate. So if the US interest rate is 5 percent, you can make a 5 percent return in one year in US dollars. Alternatively, you can buy, say, yen, invest at the yen interest rate (each currency has a different risk-free rate), and then convert back to US dollars when your riskless security matures. For this to be equal, you need something like

$$R_{usd} = R_{yen} + \text{ percent Change in yen}$$

where R_{usd} is the US interest rate, and so on.

So if you make 5 percent in USD, a US investor should receive that same return in yen by way of the interest rate in yen plus the expected appreciation or depreciation in the yen against the dollar. If the interest rate in yen is 1 percent, this means one expects the yen to appreciate against the US dollar by 4 percent. When the foreign interest rate is higher than the US interest rate, risk-neutral and rational US investors should expect the foreign currency to depreciate against the dollar by the difference between the two interest rates. This way, investors are indifferent between borrowing at home and lending abroad, or the converse. This is known as the uncovered interest rate parity condition.

The carry trade is a currency speculation strategy in which an investor borrows low-interest rate currencies and lends high-interest rate currencies, which appears to generate an abnormally high total return. This works in most cases except in the case of hyperinflation currencies. In practice, higher foreign interest rates predict that foreign currencies appreciate against the dollar, making investing in higher interest rate countries a win-win: you get appreciation on your currency and higher riskless interest rates while in that currency.

Below is the total return for a strategy that is "long" in the Australian dollar, a high-interest rate country, and borrowing (short) at the JPY interest rate. This strategy then captures the money market rates in both countries and the appreciation of the Australian dollar vis-à-vis the Japanese yen.

FIGURE 4.14. *Long AUS/short JPY carry trade total return*

Source: *Author using Bloomberg data.*

This is just one currency, and obviously you could apply this to many countries; in fact, several studies have looked at this for decades. Burnside et al. (2009) estimated a 0.99 Sharpe ratio for a strategy applied to an equally weighted basket of currencies over the period 1976–2008.

As with high returns to low-volatility stocks, it is difficult, but not theoretically impossible, to make sense of this. Robert Hodrick wrote a magisterial technical overview of currency markets in 1987. He summed up his findings in this paragraph:

We have found a rich set of empirical results. We do not yet have a model of expected returns that fit the data. International finance is no worse off in this respect than more traditional areas of finance.[101]

In other words, standard approaches looked at CAPM models, latent-variable models, conditional-variance models, models that use expenditures on durables or nondurables and services, and Kalman filters. None outperformed the spot rate as a predictor of future currency prices. Hodrick left off with the idea that "simple models may not work well." Indeed, this is true, and I think it is the ultimate hope of these researchers that a little more math will uncover a solution that is just merely complicated.

And so it continued, and many hedge funds specialized in the carry trade, which was as simple as it was successful: lend capital to high-interest rate currencies and enjoy the high riskless rates and currency appreciation of the on-the-spot rate; likewise, borrow capital at the low-interest rate currency and make money on the depreciation of this debt over time. Twenty years later, researchers had a similar conclusion:

Overall, we argue that our findings call for new theoretical macroeconomic models in which risk premia are affected by funding and liquidity constraints, not just shocks to productivity, output or the utility function.[102]

Thus the new approaches centered on "liquidity constraints," which is really like a peso problem. I am skeptical of this approach because currencies have experienced many drastic "in-sample" moves. The term "peso problem" originated in the 1970s when the Mexican government was stubbornly keeping the value of the peso fixed to the US dollar. Despite the peg, Mexican interest rates were higher than those in the United States. Economist Milton Friedman thought this was due to the market anticipating a devaluation of the peso. Yet to some, the higher interest rate spelled "free money" for those daring enough to borrow in dollars and lend in pesos. Investors reaped steady profits until markets opened on September 1, 1976, when the peso was allowed to float against the dollar. Its value plummeted more than 50 percent in one day, and many people suffered tremendous losses. Studies have been capturing peso events for decades as the carry trade contains the signature peso problem, yet the return premium remains and thus remains a puzzle to standard theory.

4.18 Corporate Bonds

The conventional corporate bond puzzle is that spreads are too high. The most conspicuous bond index captures US Baa and Aaa bond yields going back to 1919, which generates enough data to make it the corporate spread measure, especially when looking at correlations with business cycles. Yet Baa bonds are still investment grade and have only a 4.7 percent ten-year cumulative default rate after their initial rating. As the recovery rate on defaulted bonds is around 50 percent, this annualizes to a mere 0.23 percent annualized loss rate. Since the spread between Baa and Aaa bonds averaged 1.20 percent from 1919 through August 2011, this generated an approximate 0.97 percent annualized excess return compared to the riskless Aaa yield, creating the puzzle that spreads are *too high* for the risk incurred, and many researchers have approached this like the equity premium puzzle trying to explain it.

Now, the difference between Aaa and Baa may be related to something that has little to do with risk. Aaa securities get special treatment by regulators, commercial paper facilities, and as collateral for repo facilities, and so have cash-substitute qualities. Nonetheless, this is all an elite part of the credit spectrum. Only 1,000 firms worldwide carry an AAA rating.

Junk bonds, meanwhile, have default rates around 5 percent annually and are hybrids between equities and bonds because they are not merely a function of interest rates but of the stock price. In the 1980s, Michael Milken led a revolution in finance, where firms with such credit quality could have an active market, and firms could even issue bonds at this grade. Thus the data on the junk bond market really starts in the late 1980s, as before this the only junk issues were "fallen angels," and they did not trade sufficiently to have a reliable price.

Altman and Bana (2004) and Kozhemiakin (2007) noted there is no premium to high-yield portfolios relative to investment-grade portfolios, a set of bonds with a 3.84 percent average annual default rate from 1970 to 2001. Furthermore, Altman and Stonberg (2006) noted that a bankrupt bond portfolio underperforms investment-grade bonds. Both high-yield and bankrupt bonds have more volatility and cyclicality than investment-grade bonds and do their worst when returns are most valued, in bad times. Junk bonds are intuitively and empirically risky. Data from the Merrill Lynch High Yield Index show a 8.27 percent annualized return relative to the 7.63 percent return of their investment-grade index from March 1987 through December 2011. The risk premium is seen to be a modest 0.64 percent annually.

FIGURE 4.15. *Total return to Merrill Lynch US Bond Indexes: March 1987–December 2011*

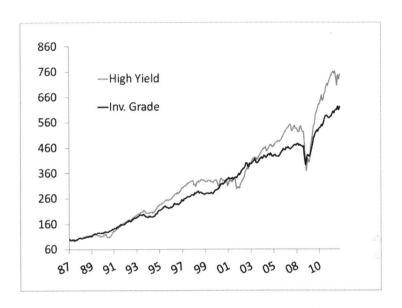

Source: *Merril Lynch.*

Yet the indexes are really an understatement of the anomaly here because of how such indexes have a systematic bias when portraying illiquid or unaudited asset classes. Even today, many times a junk bond's bid-ask spread is 5 points wide for a 70 dollar bond. Transaction costs eat away at returns derived from closing prices.

Several ETFs now allow investors access to junk and investment-grade bond returns with reasonable liquidity. The illiquidity of the ETF collateral, however, shows up in its returns. Looking at two large high-yield ETFs (JNK and HYG) and three large investment-grade ETFs (LQD, BND, and CIU) and comparing them to the Merrill Index returns over similar time periods, we see the following in figure 4.16:

FIGURE 4.16. *Actual versus index returns on bond portfolios: December 2007–December 2011*

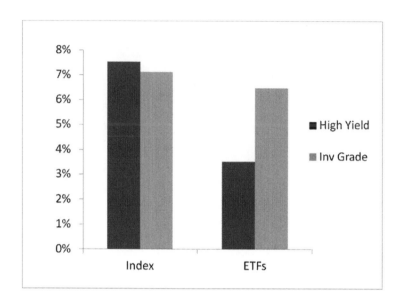

Source: *Author using Merrill Lynch and Bloomberg data.*

So both ETFs underperform the indexes, but the high-yield ETFs underperformed by quite a bit more and offset any 0.64 percent annualized premium in the indexes.

The excess corporate risk premium puzzle pertains to one portion of the risk spectrum—the difference between a 0.03 percent and a 0.3 percent annualized default rate—a distinction without a difference to most people. When one goes from a 0.3 percent to a 15 percent default rate, as one does when you go from BBB to C rated bonds, there is no risk premium within corporate bond returns. Given reasonable expectations of transaction costs, and the actual difference between the high-yield indexes and actual high-yield returns, it seems probable that people extend into higher credit risk with a lower average return.

What makes this especially puzzling is that we should remember that B and C rated companies have equity that also has lower average returns. Thus high-default-rate companies, ones that are intuitively risky, have debt that does not generate a return premium and equity that does not compensate either. It is very difficult to envisage how such risky firms generate such weak average returns in the standard model.

4.19 Yield Curve

Interest rates are probably the oldest and most liquid prices we have, and there are several facts associated with the basic default-free yield curve:

1) The real term structure is fairly flat but rises and peaks at around a three-year maturity.
2) Real rates are much more variable at the short than long end of the curve.
3) The nominal yield curve was flat prior to abandoning the gold standard in the 1930s.
4) Inflation expectations explain the majority of nominal rate fluctuations.
5) Interest rates have been pretty stationary over the past hundred years.

This latter point is especially important because it seems the short-term real rates are small (less than 1 percent and positive) over the past hundred years, though they have varied quite a bit decade to decade. Most researchers think this series is not trending. This is inconsistent with any utility function other than those with constant relative risk aversion, a special set of preferences that imply 10 percent risk to one's wealth feels the same regardless of wealth. As real GDP per capita in the United States rose 760 percent between 1900 and 2011, this seems the only logical conclusion in that framework.

The most important thing to understand with yield curves is that the high quality of US bond data since 1953 makes this sample very prominent in research, and it has a very particular pattern—rising up to 1980 then falling in concert with inflation.

As bond returns are a function of their current yield and the price appreciation from changes in market rates, the rising interest rate environment had low bond returns and the falling rate had rising ones. This leaves a tale of two regimes, and it is not clear whether the lower real returns for longer maturity bonds maturity prior to 1980, and subsequent reversal for the latter half of the sample, was an expected return or both periods were unexpected.

FIGURE 4.17. *US interest rates and inflation: 1953–2011*

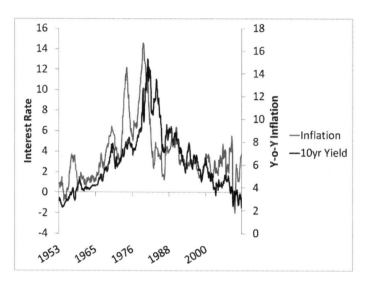

Source: *Author*

FIGURE 4.18. *Annualized return to US
Treasury yield curve for two regimes: 1954–2011*

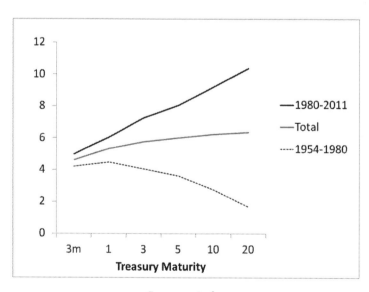

Source: *Author*

Economists were just as surprised by the movements in yields over the past sixty years as anyone else was. I worked in a bank economics department from 1987–1989, and we had no clue we were in a period of secular interest rate decline. Those same economists lamented their poor forecasts throughout the 1960s and '70s when interest rates were rising. In the 1990s, ten-year inflation-indexed yields averaged about 3.5 percent in the United Kingdom and exceeded 4 percent in the United States around 2000, declining until a spike in 2008, and currently in 2011 are below 1 percent. These movements are, in the words of Campbell, Shiller, and Viceira (2009), "a puzzle."

Keynes (1930) argued that the yield curve should slope upward due to a risk premium. Modigliani and Sutch (1966) argued that there's a habitat preference for interest rate investors so that some prefer longer bonds but most shorter durations. With the development of the stochastic discount rate factor, risk premiums are supposed to be a function of covariances with something. It isn't at all obvious what kind of covariance could explains the higher returns to longer maturity bonds post 1980, and their lower return in the 1954-1980 period. Various reasonable slices of the data give positive or negative average risk-factor loadings on plausible risk proxies. Looking at this over time perhaps shows the problem more clearly:

FIGURE 4.19. *10-year US Treasury beta with S&P 500*

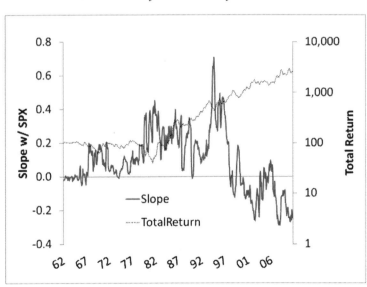

Beta from rolling 6—month daily returns to S&P500 and 10-year US Treasury
Source: *Author*

The lower returning early period and the higher returning later period do not show a clear distinction in the bond's S&P 500 factor loading, and so it is with all the various permutations of these data. The bottom line is that inflationary periods had lower bond returns than disinflationary periods have had, though it is not clear whether these are expected and thus a true risk premium or an accident. There is no obvious risk premium explanation of the default-free spectrum of bonds across maturities or time.

4.20 Futures

Futures are derivative securities, bilateral agreements to buy and sell at a future date a spot commodity at a prespecified price. Futures returns are not driven by lower expected spot prices because such prices are reflected in a low current futures price.[103] Unexpected deviations from the expected future spot price are, by definition, unpredictable and should average out to zero over time for an investor in futures, unless the investor has an ability to correctly time the market.

FIGURE 4.20. *Hypothetical backwardization versus contango in futures contracts curve*

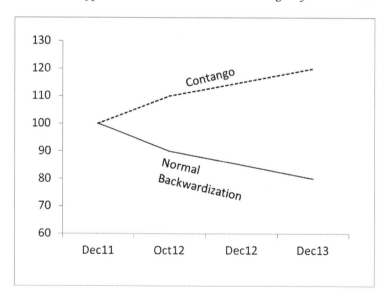

Source: *Author*

The chart above shows what normal backwardization and contango look like in futures contract charts. Historically, gold is always in contango, meaning if you are long on gold futures, you lose money on average as it rolls to maturity.

Other commodities flop around—sometimes flat, sometimes in normal back-wardization, and sometimes in contango. Erb and Harvey (2007) found that copper, heating oil, and live cattle were on average in backwardization, whereas corn, wheat, silver, gold, and coffee were in contango on average.

The expected roll returns are mainly a function of the contango/back-wardization, as the futures price empirically tends to roll toward the current spot price. This predictable return is uncorrelated with the prominent risk factors (e.g., the market, value and size factors, or the Baa-Aaa yield spread). For example, changes in inflation adversely affect the roll returns from normal back-wardization while adversely affecting the roll returns for contango.[104]

The question, obviously, is why are some futures in contango and others in normal backwardization from a risk perspective? A prominent early explanation put forth by none other than John Maynard Keynes on why futures generate risk premium from being long is that farmers grow wheat, say, and wish to hedge it by selling now rather than waiting until the season is over. A speculator who buys the wheat now and takes on the price risk, for which he must be compensated.

Futures allow operating companies to hedge their commodity price exposure, and because hedging is a form of insurance, hedgers must offer long-only commodity futures investors an insurance premium. Normal backwardation suggests that, in a world with risk-averse hedgers and investors, the excess return from a long commodity investment should be viewed as an insurance risk premium. It is easy to expand this to the other side by focusing not on the producer of a commodity, but the purchaser. Say you are Boeing and buy a lot of aluminum to build airplanes. If you hedge, you buy a futures today, locking in a price. Thus whether you hedge by buying if you are a consumer or selling if you are a producer, futures have an insurance-like characteristic. The key is knowing, between consumers and producers, who dominates the futures market for a particular contract. One explanation of the futures returns is that for some commodities, producers dominate the demand for insurance, and thus for futures; in the other, consumers dominate.

In a diversified worldwide market, however, this reasoning does not work in explaining equilibrium returns. Asset pricing theory tells us that returns are a function of risk. And as most investors are neither aluminum consumers or corn suppliers, the net covariance with the risk factor should be at work. For example, the needs of a company and its preferences are unrelated to its returns, which are a function of the change in the expectation of a company's cash flows in relation to those other things average investors care about (for example, the S&P 500). This is due to arbitrage and because asset prices are set by supply and demand, where investors should be allocating capital in a way so that the price of risk, from any source, is the same whether it comes from futures or equities. If one can get the benefits of the futures roll and not be involved in the futures commodity—as most investors are not—this should be as idiosyncratic risk is in the CAPM: diversifiable and so unpriced. And the expected roll returns, based on the current relation of the futures to the spot, are uncorrelated with the prominent risk factors for equities (that is, the market, value, and size factors) or for corporate bonds (that is, the Baa-Aaa yield spread).

There are predictable returns in futures returns, primarily from the movement in the futures price as the maturity date moves closer to the present, which is predicted in the current relation of the futures price to the spot price. What drives this, from a risk perspective, is not explained by any intuitive measure of risk (e.g., volatility or covariances).

4.21 Movies

Art DeVany and W. David Walls (2002) documented that between 1986 and 1999, G-rated movies generated lower volatility and higher returns than R-rated movies did. Data on movie returns are notoriously difficult to calculate, so they just used box-office revenue and budgets for generating a return, which DeVany estimated needs a 2 to correspond to profitable.

FIGURE 4.21. *Average return (revenue/budget) for 2,015 movies: 1985–1996*

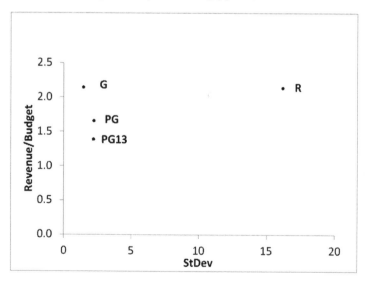

Source: *DeVany and Walls (2002)*

There was a clear preference for R-rated movies (more than a thousand R-rated movies and only sixty G-rated ones), though on a strict risk/return basis it seems that G-rated movies strictly dominated the R-rated movies, as the R-rated movies had much higher volatility. This is consistent with findings that R-rated movies have lower profits than G-rated films.[105] Popular conservative film critic Michael Medved referred to the Dove study when noting that the average G-rated film generated eight times greater profit than the average R-rated film, though R-rated films remained seventeen times more common than their G-rated counterparts. He blamed Hollywood's love for status and prestige in edgy films for trumping profits.

Aside from Hollywood status issues, movies have a strong Pareto distribution, where the mean is much higher than the median or mode. It seems everyone is betting on the next *Titanic*, because R-rated movies are the very highest grossing movies. R-rated movies are the high volatility stocks of the movie industry.

4.22 Sports Books

Since Griffith (1949), economists have known about the favorite-longshot bias: horses with the worst odds have the worst payouts. Snowberg and Wolfers (2010) looked at more than 200,000 races and reported the rate of return to betting on horses with odds of 100/1 or greater is about 61 percent, betting randomly yields average returns of 23 percent, whereas betting the favorite in every race yields losses of only around 5.5 percent. They found this bias has been persistent for fifty years at least and occurs in bookmaker, pari-mutuel, and combination markets (e.g., exacta, quiniela, and trifecta markets).

FIGURE 4.22. *Returns on horse racing by betting odds*

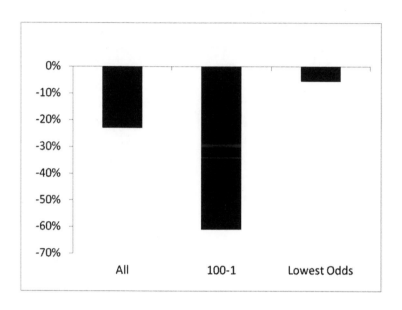

Source: *Snowberg and Wolfers (2010)*

This bias has appeared across many years and across all sizes of racetrack betting pools. The effect of these biases is that for a given fixed amount of money bet, the expected return varies with the odds level. The favorite-longshot bias is monotone across odds, and the drop-in expected value is especially large for the lower probability horses.

Interestingly, sports such as baseball and hockey, where the favorite odds are rarely greater than four to one, show no such bias. It seems the bias arises only in the extreme odds that are prevalent in horse racing but absent in most sports. That is, even a bad team has a one in four chance of winning in baseball, whereas a bad horse's chance will be more like one in fifty.

4.23. Lotteries

The annual per capita lottery expenditure in the United States is about $170, and the rate of return is about —47 percent. It clearly presents a challenge to the idea that people are looking at these games on a risk-return continuum and motivated the earliest inflected utility functions (Friedman and Savage, 1948). These investments clearly cater to what is commonly called those seeking risk, or positive skew, in particular.

Garrett and Sobel (2004) found that for the popularity (sales) of lotteries, the size of the top prize was highly significant. In other words, the $100 million super lotto has the most sales even though the probability of winning is so small it basically is outside the realm of intuition (around 1 in 150 million), and its expected return is less than -70 percent. Low payoff scratch-off bets have a 1 in 4 chance of winning, usually something like $1 to $20, but a much less disastrous −37 percent return. People who bet seem to prefer those bets that offer the worst expeted return, but the greatest maximum return, or variance. Gambling seems to be totally outside the standard assumptions of risk aversion, and has been addressed as an exception since the creation of modern aggregate utility functions.

4.24 Real Estate

Just prior to the 2008 financial crisis, there were many who thought real estate, especially residential housing, generated an above-average return. This led many to disastrously believe that the collateral of mortgage loans would always rise, making underwriting criteria irrelevant, and everything was rated too high. This is not a common assumption anymore. The Case-Shiller Index of Real Home Prices shows home prices have barely kept up with inflation, except for the bubble run-up: net real house price appreciation was minimal over the 120-year window (0.3 percent per year). Davis-Heathcote (2007) showed that for the 1930–2000 period, house prices generated a slightly higher return by about 0.5 percent, but it is in the same ballpark. Considering that utility and capital expenditures are about 2 percent per year, this implies housing is really an expense, as opposed to an investment.

The NCREIF Index of Private Real Estate Returns, which goes back to 1978 (NPNCRE Index) and is based on appraisals, is much less volatile than publicly traded REIT indexes. Although the volatility of this time series is suspect (note net asset values for close-end funds are much less variable than market values), the mean returns are useful and they show an 8.9 percent annual return relative to the S&P 500 return of 11.3 percent over the January 1978– June 2011 period. Again, if you add capital expenditures, taxes, and utilities, the returns of home ownership are probably near zero in real terms.

Looking at the US REIT Index, which includes publicly traded real estate investment trusts (REITs), we have market prices of a liquid, transparent proxy for private real estate investing. There is no direct control of the property, so it excludes some potential benefits that come from direct control but should include any costs implied from owning property, including management costs.

The FNERTR REIT Index goes back to 1975 and shows a 13.4 percent return for 1975–2011 versus 10.8 percent for the S&P 500. Interestingly, the beta for this index is about 1.3, so in some sense this fits nicely with a simple CAPM model, as REITs often contain leverage, so they could just be like a position in the S&P 500 leveraged by 30 percent.

4.25 Hedge Funds and CTAs

Hedge funds are very diverse, basically allowing managers to do whatever they want, unlike mutual funds that must be in equities and then only long. Hedge funds peaked at $2.5 trillion under management in 2007, so they are clearly significant. As funds generally receive a 2 percent asset management fee and 20 percent of the profits, I think it's clear these managers had an ability to generate above-market returns, but as usual, this does not drip back to the passive investor.

The most popular hedge fund index is the HFRI, which showed an HFR average return of 9.2 from 1990 to October 2011, 4.03 percent higher than S&P at only half the volatility (7 percent versus 15 percent). The Dow Jones Credit Suisse Hedge Fund Index outperformed the S&P 500 by 1.14 percent from January 1994 to October 2011. Thus hedge funds seem to offer above-average returns at below-average risk.

Approximately 50 percent of funds go extinct within three years, implying that the potential for bias is considerably greater than it is for equities, where we know that this was a major problem in the early version of the CRSP equity database.[106] Funds would argue that the "backfill" bias of adding the entire historical record of new funds is not really relevant to them. They maintain real-time indexes, and so if they add a fund, they will not adjust previous values based on the new fund's prior returns. Yet there is an absence of data when a fund fails, which they do admit happens. They argue that this is offset by good funds' reluctance to share data, which offsets this bias.[107]

Consider that for most hedge fund indexes, the category "Convert Arb" was taken out in 2006 after a disastrous year but returned after good performance. The index providers clearly have a vested interest in presenting good hedge fund returns and thus respond accordingly. Malkiel and Saha (2004) even found that the infamous Long Term Capital Management fund was not in databases or indexes, even though it was large, and lost 92 percent of its capital between October 1997 and October 1998.

Ibbotson, Chen, and Zhu (2010) looked at the TASS database of hedge funds from 1995– to 2009, and survivorship and backfill bias reduced returns by 6.6 percent, lower than the S&P 500 by 8.0 percent, though as mentioned, the backfill bias may not be so relevant to indexes. If one only looks at survivorship bias, the returns are reduced by 3.1 percent.

Dichev and Yu (2011) showed timing reduces fund returns by 3 percent to 7 percent using the Lipper-TASS database and the Center for International Securities and Derivatives Markets database for 11,000 funds from 1980–2008, depending on the time periods in question. As with Dichev's study on equity timing, the paper looks for the internal rate of return, dollar weighting the returns, as opposed to assuming every monthly return has the same weight. To illustrate, consider that when hedge funds peaked in 2007, they subsequently had one of their worst years; after many funds closed, hedge funds had a strong performance in 2009 with a much smaller amount of capital at work (more so than the mere loss in capital from the markdown). This asset class shows a much greater fund timing bias than for equities because hedge funds grow and shrink much more than the stock market does, where public companies are either liquidated or issue shares. Simon Lack notes that over the 1998-2010 period, a whopping 97% of the dollar profits generated by the hedge fund industry went to the fund managers, not the investors.[108] This is because the biggest decline in 2008 was when assets were at their peak.

A subset of hedge funds are commodity trading advisors (CTAs), which specialize in futures strategies that are highly liquid and represent a considerable $207B assets under management at the end of 2007. CTA performance dropped from 12.6 percent to 4.9 percent using both backfill and survivorship bias adjustments, according to Bhardwaj, Gorton, and Rouwenhorst (2008), barely above the 4 percent return on Treasury Bills from 1994 through 2007. Such accounts do, however, provide generally lower-than-equity volatility, around 10 percent annualized (versus 16 percent for the S&P 500).

4.26 Summary

In sum, the data on risk and returns does not seem consistent with any general risk premium story. The table below assigns assets classes to various high-level inferences of a risk-return pattern.

TABLE 4.10. *Asset classes and the basic risk-return nexus*

Positive Risk Premium	Zero Risk Premium	Negative Risk Premium
· Short End of Yield Curve	· Equity Country Returns	· Equities
· BBB-AAA Corporate Spread	· BBB to B Bond Return	· Betas
· Gross Equity Returns	· Futures	· Volatility
· REITs	· World Cross-sectional equity	· Minimum Variance
	· Entrepreneurial Investments	· Financial Distress
	· Private Equity	· Leverage
	· Hedge Funds	· Penny Stocks
	· CTAs	· Analyst Disagreement
	· Movies	· Options
	· Mutual Funds	· Overnight Returns
	· Housing	· IPOs and SEOs
	· Currencies	· Net Equity Return
	· Long End of Yield Curve	· Lotteries
		· Horse Racing

If one's education were unaware of utility functions, one would have to look at these data and say that volatility is inversely correlated with returns. The only clear area that a risk premium appears is in the BBB-AAA spread, the short end of the yield curve and the equity risk premium excluding taxes, survivorship bias, transaction costs, and market timing. They are exceptions to the rule, not the rule. The theory that risk proxied by intuitive concepts such as volatility, CAPM betas, or uncertainty is positively correlated with average returns fails when applied to volatility, movies, beta, developing country equities, aggregate volatility and aggregate returns, gambling, lotteries, options, financial leverage, financial distress, currencies, mutual funds, small businesses, analyst forecast dispersion, IPOs, and futures. These are not minor lacunae but the heart of the risk-return theory because they suggest any potential stochastic discount factor positively correlated with returns will be higher for firms that are intuitively safe. Even if conditional risk premia are time varying, risky characteristics are sufficiently autocorrelated to identify portfolios with greater volatility, downside tail risk, and covariance with the business cycle, and such assets with these characteristics do not have higher average returns. As a first approximation, volatility should be positively correlated with empirical returns if the risk premium is to have any meaning in an asset pricing theory.

CHAPTER 5

Relative Status
Utility and Risk Premiums

The data presented generate the following general pattern across volatility for your average asset class.

FIGURE 5.1. *Expected utility as a function of volatility*

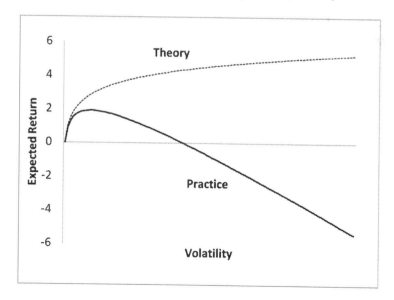

Although volatility is not risk, volatility is positively correlated with covariances of anything that could be risk: betas with the market, with the business cycle, and other factors. If this graph is reality, these are not only average returns but also expected returns. The purpose here is to look at models that explain this. This is derivative of earlier work I have presented in Falkenstein (2009, 2009b).

5.1 The General Theory of Relative Status Asset Pricing

This is best illustrated by the following simple model. If you hate equations, you can get the essence of how relative oriented utility functions eliminate risk premiums with this simple example illustrated by Table 5.1 and then skip to chapter 6. There are two assets, X and Y, and two states of nature, 1 and 2. An investor faced with asset X or Y can see the following returns:

TABLE 5.1. *Payoffs to assets X and Y in states 1 and 2*

	Total Return		Avg.	Relative Return	
	X	Y		X	Y
State 1	0	−10	−5	5	−5
State 2	20	30	25	−5	5

As shown in the table above, Y is conventionally considered riskier, with a 40-point range in payoffs versus a 20-point range for X. Yet on a relative basis, each asset generates identical risk. In State 1, X is a +5 out performer; in State 2, X is a -5 underperformer, and vice versa for asset Y. In relative return space, the higher absolute volatility asset is not riskier; the reader can check this for any example in which the two assets have the same mean absolute payout over the states (i.e., the average for asset X and asset Y is the same). The risk in low-volatility assets is its losing ground during good times. If X and Y are the only two assets in the economy, equivalent relative risk can be achieved by taking on an undiversified bet on X or Y, which is identical to taking a position on not-Y and not-X. The positions, from a relative standpoint, are mirror images. Meanwhile, buying the market—in this case, allocating half of each—generates zero risk.

Everything in the idea that a risk premium for relative utility environments is zero flows from this simple model. Implicitly, the equilibrium and arbitrage solutions come from the fact that when relative portfolio wealth is the argument in the utility function, *systematic* volatility is symmetric, as the complement to any portfolio subset will necessarily have identical—though opposite signed—relative return. If utility is relative, gains from trade can always be made if there is a risk premium.

5.2 Equilibrium with Relative Utility

Consider a two-period economy with two identical individuals, i and $-i$. There are two types of assets—one is a risk-free bond that pays off R_f with certainty in Period I. There also exists an equity with a return of R_E, where

$$R_E \sim N\left(\mu, \sigma^2\right) \tag{5.1}$$

Total wealth for the individual i in period 0 is given by his portfolio of assets.

$$w_i^0 = \alpha_E^i R_E + \alpha_f^i R_F \tag{5.2}$$

α_E^i and α_f^i represent the holdings for investor i on the risky and risk-free asset, respectively. Each individual is endowed with k units of wealth, so the budget constraint is

$$w_i^0 \leq k \tag{5.3}$$

Agent i's utility function is driven by his wealth relative to the other agent (there is no consumption) in an exponential utility function with a risk aversion coefficient a.

$$U_i\left(w_i^1 - w_{-i}^1\right) = -\exp\left(-a\left\{w_i^1 - w_{-i}^1\right\}\right) \tag{5.4}$$

As the argument in equation (5.4) is normally distributed, the individual, therefore, maximizes the following certainty equivalent function:[109]

$$\underset{\alpha_E^i, \alpha_f^i}{Max} \; E\left(w_i^1 - w_{-i}^1\right) - \frac{a}{2} Var\left(w_i^1 - w_{-i}^1\right) \tag{5.5}$$

Note his utility is strictly increasing in his own wealth, w^I_i and strictly decreasing in the wealth of the other investor, w^I_{-i}, reflecting the relative status/ envy in this economy. Also the variance of his difference from this other investor negatively impacts his utility in an amount proportional to his coefficient of risk aversion, a. As there is no consumption, the agent can do nothing to affect his period 0 wealth, so his relevant decision only concerns optimizing for period 1. His utility is strictly increasing in α_E and α_f, so his budget constraint holds with equality; from equations (5.2), and (5.3) we have

$$\alpha^i_f = k - \alpha^i_E \tag{5.6}$$

Substituting for w^I_i and w^I_{-i} and applying the expectations operator, this problem expands to

$$\underset{\alpha^i_E}{Max}\ \alpha^i_E \mu + \left(k - \alpha^i_E\right)R_f\ -\alpha^{-i}_E \mu\ -\left(k - \alpha^{-i}_E\right)R_f\ -\frac{a\sigma^2}{2}\left(\alpha^i_E - \alpha^{-i}_E\right)^2 \tag{5.7}$$

Taking the first order conditions with respect to α^i_E, we have

$$\mu = R_f + a\sigma^2\left(\alpha^i_E - \alpha^{-i}_E\right) \tag{5.8}$$

Because each agent is identical, in equilibrium each agent holds the same amount.

$$\alpha^i_E = \alpha^{-i}_E \tag{5.9}$$

Given equations (5.8) and (5.9), we have

$$\mu = R_f \tag{5.10}$$

Remember that μ here in equation (5.10) is from equation (5.1), the mean return on the 'risky' asset in this model. As there is no β and no risk aversion coefficient a in equation (5.10), the same expected return holds regardless of its sensitivity to the market factor r_m or the volatility of the market, σ. The returns on all assets—low risk, high risk, no risk—are the same. Risk does not affect return in equilibrium.

The model allows a strict comparison to the traditional case, where there is no peer comparison in the argument of the utility function. If instead of a relative utility function a traditional von Neumann-Morgenstern utility function based on absolute wealth is used, such as

$$U_i\left(w_i^1\right) = -\exp\left(-aw_i^1\right) \tag{5.11}$$

then using the same reasoning above generates the traditional result that riskiness affects returns, specifically,

$$\underset{\alpha_E^i,\alpha_f^i}{Max}\ \mathrm{E}\left(w_i^1\right)-\frac{a}{2}Var\left(w_i^1\right) \tag{5.12}$$

Substituting for w^1_i using equation (5.6) we have

$$\underset{\alpha_E^i}{Max}\ \alpha_E^i\mu +\left(k-\alpha_E^i\right)R_f\ -\frac{a\sigma^2}{2}\left(\alpha_E^i\right)^2 \tag{5.13}$$

Differentiating with respect to $\alpha_E^{\,i}$ we have the traditional results that the return on risky assets is greater than for risk-free assets, return is strictly increasing in the volatility of the market (σ^2), the risk aversion coefficient (a), and the amount of the risky asset the individuals holds $(\alpha_E^{\,i})$.

$$\mu = R_f + a\sigma^2\alpha_E^i \tag{5.14}$$

Again, here μ is the mean return on the risky, asset, but in this case we get the standard result, as in Merton (1980), that the expected return of the nondiversifiable risky asset is a linear function of its variance. In both the traditional and the relative risk scenarios above, identical optimizing agents hold the same amount of each asset because they are identical; however, asset prices are different in the two scenarios, so that there exists a zero risk-return relation when individuals have relative status utility functions, whereas in the traditional case, higher nondiversifiable volatility increases the expected return for risk. The intuition is that in the traditional approach, nondiversifiable risks diminishes expected utility, so this undesired aspect of an asset lowers its price to make it comparable in marginal utility per dollar with the safe asset. In contrast, in the relative status model, 'risk' can be avoided entirely by choosing symmetric portfolios, which individuals do in equilibrium in order to maximize their joint utility.

5.3 Arbitrage with Relative Utility

Of course, this same result comes out of an arbitrage approach as well. Assume an economy with risky assets that are a function of a market factor r_m. For any investor i who chooses an asset with a specific beta β_i returns are generated via the factor model

$$r_i = \mu_{\beta_i} + \beta_i r_m \tag{5.15}$$

Where μ_{β_i} is a constant for an asset with the specific beta β_i and $r_m \sim N(\mu_m, \sigma_m^2)$. We will assume no idiosyncratic risk from assets because the gist of this approach is without loss of generality (i.e., idiosyncratic risk would be optimally diversified away in any large economy). The return on the risk-free asset is the constant r_f. We are solving for a r_f, μ_{β_i} and μ_m such that this is an equilibrium.

The market return in this model is the benchmark to which investors compare themselves, just as mutual fund managers typically try to outperform their benchmark. Their objective is to maximize their out performance, subject to minimizing its variance. Define r_{out}^i as the relative performance of investor i to the market return

$$r_{out}^i = r_i - r_m \tag{5.16}$$

Here r_i is the return on the investor's portfolio with its particular factor loading β_i and r_m is the return on the market. Investors all have the simple objective of maximizing r_{out}^i while minimizing a proportion of its variance, as in

$$Max \ r_{out}^i - \frac{a}{2}\sigma_i^2 \tag{5.17}$$

Where $\sigma^2_i = Var(r_i - r_m)$. Substituting equation (5.15) into (5.16) generates

$$r^i_{out} = \mu_{\beta_i} + (\beta_i - 1)r_m \tag{5.18}$$

Because r_m is the only random variable, the variance of outperformance is just

$$\sigma^2_i = (\beta_i - 1)^2 \sigma^2_m \tag{5.19}$$

Equation (5.19) implies that the beta bet is risky to the extent it deviates from the average in either direction. We can replicate the relevant risk of a stock with a beta of β_i via a portfolio consisting of β_i units of the market portfolio and investing/borrowing $(1-\beta_i)$ units of the risk-free asset. Arbitrage then implies that these have the same expected returns, so

$$E\left(\beta_i r_m + (1 - \beta_i)r_f\right) = E\left(\mu_{\beta_i} + \beta_i r_m\right) \tag{5.20}$$

The LHS of equation (5.20) is the market portfolio levered β_i times by investing/borrowing $(1-\beta_i)$ in the risk-free asset in financing, whereas the RHS is the unlevered β_i asset portfolio via equation (5.15). They have the same factor exposure and cost the same, so they should have the same return in equilibrium. Thus equation (5.20) implies

$$\mu_{\beta_i} = (1 - \beta_i)r_f \tag{5.21}$$

This allows us to replace the μ_{β_i} with $(1-\beta_i) \cdot r_f$ in equation (5.18) and leads to the factor model

$$r^i_{out} = (1 - \beta_i)r_f + (\beta_i - 1)r_m \tag{5.22}$$

If the degree of risk relevant to investors is their out performance, σ^i_2, the expected return for assets with $\beta = k$ should be the same as those with $\beta = 2-k$ because they have the same risk in this environment: $(k-1)^2\sigma^2_m = ((2-k)-1)^2\sigma^2_m$.

The risk of a $\beta = k$ asset is identical in magnitude to a $\beta = (2-k)$ asset in this model, so the expected returns must be the same via arbitrage:

$$E\left(r^i_{out} \mid \beta = k\right) = E\left(r^i_{out} \mid \beta = 2 - k\right) \tag{5.23}$$

Using equation (5.22) and (5.23) on the equivalence of $2-k$ and k beta assets, and applying the expectations operator, we have

$$(1-k)r_f + (k-1)E(r_m) = (1-(2-k))r_f + ((2-k)-1)E(r_m) \tag{5.24}$$

The LHS of equation (5.24) is the expected return on the $\beta = k$ asset, and the RHS is the expected return on the $\beta = 2-k$ asset. Solving for $E(r_m)$, we get

$$E(r_m) = r_f \tag{5.25}$$

Equations (5.15), (5.21), and (5.25) imply

$$\begin{aligned} r_i &= r_f + \beta_i\left(r_m - r_f\right) \\ r_m &\sim N\left(r_f, \sigma_m\right) \end{aligned} \tag{5.26}$$

Thus no arbitrage, in the sense things equivalent in risk are priced the same (as risk is defined here), generates the traditional CAPM with the significant difference that the expected market return is equivalent to the risk-free rate. Just as the equilibrium model in the prior section implies, the expected return on all assets is the same because $E\beta_i(r_m - r_f) = 0 \; \forall \; \beta_i$.

In contrast, a traditional arbitrage model would start from the equivalence of risk in a β_i asset and a portfolio levered in the market by borrowing $(\beta_i - 1)$ into the risky asset. These have the same portfolio risk $\beta_i^2\sigma^2$:

$$E\left(\beta_i r_m + (1-\beta_i)r_f\right) = E\left(\mu_{\beta_i} + \beta_i r_m\right) \tag{5.27}$$

Solving for μ_{β_i} and applying back to the equation (5.15), we have the standard factor model

$$E(r_i) = r_f + E\beta_i(r_m - r_f) \tag{5.28}$$

Here the maximization function reflects the fact that the investor cares only about absolute volatility, not volatility relative to some benchmark.

$$\underset{\beta_i}{Max} \quad r^i - \frac{a}{2}\beta_i^2\sigma_m^2 \tag{5.29}$$

Substituting equation (5.28) for r_i, the first order condition for choosing beta on equation (5.29) generates the familiar equation

$$\beta_i = \frac{E(r_m - r_f)}{a\sigma_m^2} \tag{5.30}$$

So investor i's optimal β_i will be equal to the risk premium over the risk aversion coefficient times the market variance. Assuming a representative investor, conventional parameters for this approach of 3 percent for the risk premium, 3 for a risk coefficient, and 10 percent for market volatility, this implies an equilibrium beta choice of 1, consistent with an equilibrium where the representative investor holds the market basket. The numbers are not a perfect empirical match, but they show that they are reasonably close to fitting reality. But if, as argued above in Chapter 4, the market premium is in effect zero for the marginal investor, the β_i choice would be zero in this model, which would not be an equilibrium because on average the market beta is 1 by definition and in positive net supply. In the traditional approach, a positive market premium is necessary for investors to hold the market in equilibrium.

In contrast, the relative status approach generates the following maximization objective:

$$\underset{\beta_i}{Max} \quad (1 - \beta_i)r_f + \beta_i r_m - \frac{a}{2}(\beta_i - 1)^2\sigma_m^2 \tag{5.31}$$

Which produces the following equilibrium relation:

$$\beta_i = \frac{E(r_m - r_f)}{a\sigma_m^2} + 1 \tag{5.32}$$

Here the optimal choice of β_i is 1 only if the risk premium is zero (i.e., $E[r_m] = r_f$) because risk is uncompensated via arbitrage, and risk can be avoided in this model by choosing a beta of 1. A positive risk premium would induce a desired optimal beta greater than 1, which would then not be an equilibrium.

This simple model has no more simplicity than what generates traditional risk premiums. Assumptions drive results, which makes both models trivial in a sense (i.e., as with any math, it's trivial once you know it). The only difference is whether one puts relative as opposed to absolute wealth in the utility function. Both the absolute- and relative-risk approach generate the familiar factor pricing model, but in the relative-risk approach the risk premium is zero in equilibrium, whereas in the absolute-risk approach the risk premium must be positive.

5.4 The Low Return to High-Risk Assets

While as a first approximation, a zero risk-return relationship seems appropriate, there also appears to be clear evidence that often the highest risk assets have lower-than-average, even negative, returns. An interesting point is that the relative-utility approach can accommodate this fact, where the standard approach would need some ad hoc restrictions. The starting point is to first assume that there are many people who prefer volatile assets for some reason. There are several reasons why people invest in these risky investments—higher risk, lower return—and they are examined in Chapter 7, but for now just assume there is a significant, exogenous demand for these assets.

In a standard model, if some investors push up prices on riskier-than-average assets, resulting in those assets having lower-than-average returns, rational investors would simply avoid if not short them. The marginal investor would set the price, and so with short-selling, irrespective of how much the delusional, volatility-loving asset buyers bought, returns would be unaffected by their demand. This is contradicted by the data in that most investors hold low returning risky positions as part of their portfolios via index funds and mutual funds that hold such assets; most equity investors hold these assets in positive amounts, either directly or indirectly.

Consider the following asset demand equation that results from the standard model above and is common in asset pricing theory (rearranged from 5.14).

$$\alpha_E^i = \frac{\mu - R_f}{a\sigma^2} \tag{5.33}$$

Whereas in the relative utility case (rearranged from 5.8), the same demand function is of the following form:

$$\alpha_E^i = \frac{\mu - R_f}{a\sigma^2} + \alpha_E^{-i} \tag{5.34}$$

In the first case, the standard approach, investor demand, is indifferent to the demand of other investors. Demand is strictly a function of the *excess* return scaled by the risk in this model and his risk preference parameter. If an asset has a zero excess return but some positive level of risk, his demand is zero; if the risky asset's return is below the risk-free rate, the demand is for a short position. In contrast, the relative utility investor still can hold positive amounts in equilibrium even if the expected return on the asset is negative because, from equation (5.34) we see that

$$\alpha_E^i > 0 \text{ if } \frac{\mu - R_f}{a\sigma^2} > -\alpha_E^{-i} \tag{5.35}$$

In the relative utility as shown in equation (5.35), rational investors simply make room for poor assets and hold them in positive amounts even though they could have returns below the risk-free rate or even negative. In the absolute utility case, rational investors should be shorting those with negative returns, and for all the really highly volatile equities, this is definitely not the case empirically, as mainstream investors appear indifferent to their index funds that hold such volatile assets by necessity. Benchmarking investors are wary of missing out, even if that hurts their absolute returns. People willingly hold volatile, low-returning assets in this framework, where they would not if they had standard utility functions. Also note that investors will hold only more than average amounts of some asset if such an asset has a higher-than-average expected return.

5.5 Academic Precedence

Several prominent academics have accepted the fact that high volatility assets *can* have lower-than-average returns, and so it remains for theorists to make this consistent with a model. They draw on a basic premise in my model, that relatively oriented utility functions vastly change the risk premium. In a sense, like any good idea, it can be seen within the existing literature; my only novelty being one of asserting its generality.

An early paper by Abel (1990) showed that if people were interested in the consumption relative to prior periods (habit persistence) or prior aggregate consumption (the "catching-up-with-the-Joneses"), the spread between the expected return premium for stocks and the risk-free rate diminished considerably, potentially explaining the seemingly too high equity premium puzzle.[110] His utility function was of the form

$$U(c_t, C_{t-1}) = (1-\alpha)^{-1} \left({c_t}/{C_{t-1}} \right)^{1-\alpha} \tag{5.36}$$

Where the little c is the per individual consumption, and the big C is aggregate consumption. By normalizing an individual's consumption using last period's aggregate consumption, the implicit relative variation in consumption rises significantly, amplifying the perceived risk of one's portfolio. This is a hedonic treadmill effect, so that every period a new benchmark level is set. This also works by lowering the implied risk-free rate because the growth in consumption over time is eliminated via the updated benchmark.

Gali (1995) expanded this so that aggregate (C) and individual (c) consumption have independent exponents:

$$U(c, C) = (1-a)^{-1} c^{1-a} C^{\gamma a} \tag{5.37}$$

Unlike Abel, this uses contemporaneous consumption and adds a parameter that can amplify or offset the risk of an individual. If $\gamma > 0$, there are public goods aspects to aggregate consumption, as when your neighbors spend their money on making your neighborhood more beautiful. If $\gamma < 0$, people are incented to "keep up with the Joneses," as when everyone gets a new flat-screen TV, and now your otherwise perfectly working but old-fashioned TV seems much less enjoyable. The idea was to show that externalities, always a popular model refinement, can conspire to make aggregate risk aversion preferences even less measurable, because now there are multiple risk preference/externality parameters consistent with any data.

In DeMarzo, Kaniel, and Kremer (2004), the utility function is not assumed but rather endogenous. They presented a model where agent's utility is a function of two types of consumption: standard goods and positional goods. Positional goods are things such as mates, beachfront properties, or table seatings at a trendy restaurant, whose supply is unaffected by aggregate wealth. They create a complete model by having the positional goods proxied by service consumption in period 2 provided by a fixed amount of labor, so that regardless of the total wealth in the model, people will be competing for access to services in exactly the same way. Thus the positional nature of the service goods is endogenous to the model. Their utility function is given by

$$U\left(c_g, c_s\right) = \left(1-a\right)^{-1}\left(c_g^{1-a} + c_s^{1-a}\right) \tag{5.38}$$

Here, a is the standard coefficient of risk aversion, c_g the consumption of goods, c_s the consumption of services. Total output for the economy is a function of a fixed amount of services (e.g., the same number of barbers regardless of societal wealth) and a random production from the risky asset (the technology shock). As the production of services, c_s, is fixed by the size of the labor pool and unaffected by the output from risky investment, the relative size of the positional goods market, due to services, can lead to lower than otherwise risk premiums. Thus the services market is like a relative status economy because the aggregate wealth here does not effect it—that is, people are fighting over a fixed pie. One can think of the case where all the weighting is on the consumption of positional goods, and then you have the utility function I specified, where the argument is a purely relative consumption amount.

DeMarzo, Kaniel, and Kremer suggested this is relevant to bubbles because the risk premium *can* become zero or negative. Yet they stressed the mere possibility, and so like any equation that adds more terms, this model explains more when relying on the additional positional good, but it remains an exercise for the reader to determine if this applies to, say, Internet stocks in 2000.

Similarly, Roussanov (2010) had a model with a utility function each period of

$$\frac{C^{1-a}}{1-a} + \eta \bar{W}_s^{1-a}\left(\frac{W^i_s}{\overline{W}_s}\right) \tag{5.39}$$

Where C is consumption, W is wealth, and the agent is comparing his wealth (W^i_s) to others ($\bar{W}_s$) in the second term, similar to in my model (relative wealth). Roussanov found that for certain values of η, the model predicts low, even negative, expected returns. Embedding the relative wealth idea within a conventional model makes it easier for academics to digest, but the generality make the results ambiguous, given parameterizations of η.

These models highlight that my logic is correct, that a relative status orientation can lower the risk premia to zero and below. My main innovation is merely to make this connection less subtle, tentative, and convoluted. In those papers, the main innovation was basically to show that adding a "relative wealth/consumption term" alters risk premiums on some assets in some scenarios. It can increase them, or decrease them, and there are various plausible rationalizations for either (keeping up with the Joneses, positional goods, negative externalities).

The key is which utility function best explains the world we see, and a relative status one works much better than a standard one based on decreasing marginal utility of absolute consumption. To add a parameter that captures the fact that *some* consumption is of positional goods and assert this *can* create different risk premia, merely highlights that smart people are very good at rationalizing anomalies by adding complexity. It does not predict; it merely explains. The main point I wish to make is that if people are better defined as benchmarking and not greedy, theoretically this leads to zero risk premiums, which is generally what we observe.

5.6 Uncertainty and Fat Tails

I was a teaching assistant for Hyman Minsky while an undergrad at Washington University. Minsky was a leading post-Keynesian economist. His big idea was that risk was the fundamental difference between his post-Keynesian school and orthodox economics. In his mind, mainstream economists trivialized risk, packed it into a hermetically sealed irrelevance, and made it a cost no different than the price of wheat. In Minsky's conception, risk was this wonderfully elusive, powerful concept. It was why markets may work with consumption goods within a prison camp but why they fail when dealing with large-scale investment projects. He considered, of course, Keynes to be the source of his understanding of risk, which is "that which cannot be quantified." There was something indubitably right about the incalculability of real-world events, in contrast to explicit games of chance.

Keynes stated in his 1937 *Quantitative Journal of Economics* article:

By "uncertain" knowledge, let me explain, I do not mean merely to distinguish what is known for certain from what is merely probable. The game of roulette is no subject, in this sense, to uncertainty; nor is the prospect of a Victory bond being drawn. Or, again, the expectation of life is only slightly uncertain. Even the weather is only moderately uncertain. The sense in which I am using the term is that in which the prospect of an European war is uncertain, or the price of copper and the rate of interest twenty years hence or the obsolescence of a new invention, or the position of private wealth owners in the social system in 1970. About these matters there is no scientific basis on which to form any calculable probability whatever. We simply do not know.[111]

Frank Knight's definition is functionally the same, that risk is measurable randomness, and uncertainty relates to immeasurable randomness where one has enough information to form an opinion, but not to have an objective probability. The confusion arises because opinions on the future have the same form as an explicit probability.[112]

L.J. Savage (1954) argued you can model these uncertain estimates as if they were true probabilities, and as a modeler there was really no alternative, so people basically jumped on this idea without much regret. Experiments have shown that many individuals do not behave in a manner consistent with subjective expected utility, most prominently in the Allais (1953) and Ellsberg (1961) paradoxes, but these are seen as strange exceptions.

The main problem with this vein of thinking is that, invariably, volatility and covariances are highly correlated with an intuitive metric of uncertainty, fat tails, and imprecision. The uncertainty or imprecision around a low-volatility stock is surely less than for a highly volatile stock. Indeed, when we measure uncertainty directly, as in analyst forecast dispersion, we see the exact same results as we do when we measure volatility or beta: higher risk/uncertainty leads to lower cross-sectional equity returns. In practice, the uncertainty distinction is redundant to volatility or covariance estimates.

Weitzman (2007) or Bansal and Yaron (2004) looked at cases where one is learning about the true stochastic process with finite data, and given some assumptions about the underlying stochastic process, basically makes the data seem to have very fat tails prospectively. Obviously, it solves the equity premium puzzle because risk is much greater than any simple sample volatility, and is related to a lot of similar issues related to fat tails and peso problems.[113] Generally, assets with large conditional probabilities of highly adverse events, such as when the peso was devalued or when equity prices jump downward by

50 percent, also have high volatility. Researchers have shown how these concerns can explain the equity premium puzzle, which I would argue is not nearly as large as these people think, but in any case it then fails miserably to explain why the risk premium within asset classes is generally flat, often negative.

CHAPTER 6

Why Envy Explains More than Greed

The finding that a relative utility function can explain the general absence of a risk premium could be merely explaining a subset of the applications utility function are applied to. The power of the relative utility approach should be evident in other spheres as well, and this is helpful in assessing whether it is more fruitful, and here I think the evidence is very strong for the relative utility case. The key is moving from a utility function solely focused on one's own wealth (aka greed) to one focused on relative wealth (aka envy).

First note that individuals attempting to maximize their wealth or relative standing often behaves quite similarly; in both cases, one wants to increase one's wealth. The incentive to economize on purchases or maximize their profits and avoid random adversities would be the same under the assumption of absolute or relative wealth maximization.

6.1 Robust Hard Wiring

It's important to note that evolution favors a relative utility function as opposed to the standard absolute utility function, and the evidence for this is found in psychology, ethology, anthropology, and neurology.

A major difference in these conceptions of utility arises looking at the evolution of agents over generations. The instinctive utility that guides individual decisions under all time periods is presumably the same. If a person experiences an increase in wealth, the fact as to whether he will decrease, keep unchanged, or increase the fraction of his portfolio invested in risky assets depends on whether his relative risk aversion is decreasing, constant, or increasing, respectively. It seems reasonable to assume the fraction of investor portfolios allocated to risky assets has remained stable over time, which implies using a constant relative risk aversion (CRRA) utility function, as in $U(c) = \frac{c^{1-a}}{1-a}$, which may look funny but has the nice property of having risk aversion be *relatively* constant—that is, they bet in similar magnitudes proportional to their current wealth. This is necessary if real interest rates are constant over the past century, as most researchers believe.

Most economists think that reasonable parameters for the relative risk aversion coefficient, *a*, are between 1 and 10, most commonly a number between 1.5 and 3. This specific utility function is necessary so that when we think of a risky investment today, it means about the same thing as a risky investment to our grandparents.

The problem created by such a function has bizarre generalizations. Matthew Rabin highlighted that *any* risk-averse utility function extrapolates poorly. He proved that any person who turns down wagers where he stands to lose $100 or

FIGURE 6.1. *Utility as a function of income, CCRA with a = 1.5*

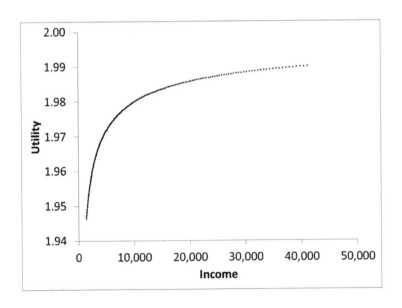

gain $110, each with 50 percent probability, must also turn down 50–50 bets of losing $1,000 or gaining any sum of money. This is clearly absurd, because for a million or a billion dollars, hardly any rational person would do this. You can see this by looking at the following graph.

The curvature of the utility function necessary and sufficient for a risk premium implies much less of a distinction as one increases income (or consumption or wealth or whatever you put in the utility function). The downside is so much more curved than the upside that the differences in utility on the upside basically become indistinguishable above a certain point, where having $1 million or $1 billion would feel the same to someone currently with only $10,000. As average income has risen fivefold in the past hundred years, any current 50 percent fluctuation in income would seem imperceptible to our great-grandparents (assuming they had standard utility function preferences). Yet clearly, currently we really do care when our income halves or doubles, a lot more than our great-grandparents could empathize with.

Assume you are the Intelligent Designer of a species of conscious agents, or the program developer of agents in some kind of SimCity (some philosophers seriously consider the possibility we are simply avatars in some higher dimensional game as in *The Matrix*, see Bostrom [2003]). The objective you face is to give these agents a goal, such that they are motivated to be fruitful and multiply over generations. As the designer, you can add a mechanism so that agents feel hungry if low on calories and lustful when in the presence of mating opportunities so they survive over generations. Yet each of these desires needs to have a clear governor that has a satiation setting too; you don't want these agents eating or having sex so much they ignore everything else, such as taking care of their children, nor do you want them to engage in these necessary desires to excess, say becoming obese. Now consider that there is a governor that signals the desire to want more "stuff", which ensures that these beings don't become lazy and unproductive once basic levels of material wants are satisfied, even though compared to average wealth at the start of their existence, they are all fabulously wealthy compared to ancestors five generations prior.

If a human's guide is solely based on their individual consumption irrespective of everyone else, the agent must have a very specific utility function. If this function is misspecified just a little bit it would lead to disaster as the economy grows or shrinks over generations. The CRRA utility function is needed so we allocate about the same amount of our wealth to risky assets over generations but implies we should be at a much higher level of happiness relative to our grandparents, which seems counterfactual (see section 6.2 below on the

Easterlin paradox). A solution that would generate a more stable level of overall happiness, and still incent them to better themselves, would be to have a little governor that simply says try to be above average, to have a higher percentile of wealth among your peers. Desire has no near bliss point but a more reasonable feedback mechanism that does not lead to an absurdity.

Economists Rayo and Becker (2007) literally invoked the designer approach to relative utility, but as economists and not philosophers, they cast it as a principal-agent problem, where the principal is in the role of the designer and the agent is the avatar.[114] A relative-status utility function is more of an evolutionary stable strategy than an absolute function because it is much more robust as societies change from hunter gatherer tribes, to stasis after the development of agriculture, to persistent economic growth in Western countries since around 1750.

A utility function focused on absolute levels of wealth would need context-dependent granularity over time, the way eyes are fit for one part of the light spectrum but not others. For example, the wave lengths humans see are by necessity only a small fraction of what is possible. For specific historical reasons humans have three types of visual cells called cones that detect wave lengths centered at 450 nm, 550 nm, and 600 nm, which we call blue, green, and red, and their combination of intensity gives us the qualia we call color. If for some reason wavelengths outside this spectrum became important for survival, we would have to evolve new cone types capable of distinguishing, say, the 900 nm versus 1100 nm wave length. This would be a costly evolutionary adjustment to our architecture, not a mere extension of what is already there.[115]

In a similar way, our sensitivity to wealth would be much more robust if we made sure agents merely monitor their relative output, not absolute. This way as the environment becomes wealthier the lens that rank orders the effect of choices on one's happiness does not need constant adjustment. Like God setting up the laws of the universe and letting them run, here the designer merely has humans want to do better than their peers, and they will continue to build, create, and multiply regardless of the technology shocks they face. The alternative seems much more problematic, in that if our great-grandparent merely wants a nice shack, it would take some major adjustment to get that same species to want a 3000 square foot house vs. the 1500 square foot houses common a generation ago.

Biologists Insel and Fernald (2004) argued that because information about social status is essential for reproduction and survival, specialized neural mechanisms have evolved to process social information, making status orientation hardwired into our brains as a consequence of evolutionary selection (mates are the ultimate status item). Neurologists have done experiments and found thinking about other people is biologically concentrated in a specific area of the brain (the right temporo-parietal junction), and damaging this region diminishes one's ability to empathize and this is profoundly debilitating.[116] As one neurologist notes in explaining a popular optical illusion, 'we can't not see context.'[117] In the late 1980s, researchers discovered mirror neurons that fire both when an animal acts and when the animal observes the same action performed by another.[118] This is tied to the incessant mimicry in humans, as when babies stick out their tongue if their mother sticks out her tongue. Neuroscience researcher Naomi Eisenberger puts in this way, "Most processes operating in the background when your brain is at rest are involved in thinking about other people and yourself."[119] Thinking relatively and socially is hardwired.

In the book *I'll Have What She's Having*, the anthropologist authors argue that we mostly copy everyone else: first our parents, then our peers, then anyone who seems to be doing well. Generally, it works, as if you want to figure out how to ride the subway, you could do worse than stand back and watch everyone else. Evolutionary biologist Mark Pagel takes this a step further by stating emulating others is the basis for almost every idea we have, and notes that very few of us create things that are later used by many others; think the number zero, the wheel, soap.[120] A strategy of simply surveying and taking the best ideas dominates the strategy of solving these problems ourselves. We are fundamentally an imitating species.[121]

Most innovators spend their formative years producing derivative work: Bob Dylan's first album contained 11 cover songs, comedian Richard Pryor began his career doing imitations of Bill Cosby, and most professors published their first paper by merely extending their dissertation advisor's ideas. We copy to acquire knowledge that becomes the foundation for variations and extensions that appear to outsiders as 'thinking outside the box.'

If we are constantly emulating others and attempting to merely outperform our neighbors, this leads to a status-oriented utility function. While used only piecemeal in standard economic theory, anthropologist Dan Brown documented a concern for status (what I am calling envy) as a "human universal"—whereas greed is not.[122] Status relates to longevity and health, even when factors such as income and education are controlled for.[123] Famous economists such as Adam Smith, Karl Marx, Thorstein Veblen, and even Keynes focused on status, the societal relative position, as a motivating force in individual lives.[124] Lastly, greed and envy are in the seven deadly sins, but envy is more prominent in the Ten Commandments. My pitch for envy over greed is hardly novel.

6.2 The Easterlin Paradox

A fundamental problem with the standard utility functions is that although they imply a constant sense of relative riskiness as wealth per capita grows, happiness should be increasing fairly significantly. The Easterlin paradox (1974) highlighted that although within a society rich people are happier than poor people, rich countries are not much happier than poor countries, and, further, as a population gets richer, they do not get happier.

A good example of this is Japan, where per capita income rose 500 percent from 1958 through 1987, yet there was little change in subjective well-being. Chinese real income has risen 250 percent from 1994 through 2006, and surveyed happiness actually declined.[125] Most Western countries experienced 200 percent growth in per capita income from 1960 through 2007, without any obvious increase in happiness. This striking fact has led to many books such as Easterbrook's *The Progress Paradox*, David Myers's *The American Paradox*, and Barry Schwartz's *The Paradox of Choice*, all focused on the seeming paradox at work here. Wealth does not appear to be the simple producer of happiness many thought it was.

Meanwhile, there has been much documentation that relative wealth, not absolute wealth, is preferred. Imagine a world where you can earn $100k in perpetuity while others earn $90k, and one where you earn $110k while others earn $200k. Which would you choose? Most people prefer to live in the poorer world where there are relatively wealthier.[126] Researchers have found that Chinese villagers were more affected by relative wealth than by absolute wealth. Studies using functional magnetic resonance imaging (fMRI) to monitor brain activity found that social context is an important factor in processing rewards.[127] As Robert Frank noted in his book *The Darwin Economy*, this makes evolutionary sense in that if we are primarily concerned with positional goods—such as lakefront housing, mates, or status—no amount of extra wealth is going to affect aggregate supply because it is all a zero-sum game.

It is important to note that Wolfers and Stevenson (2008) dispute the assertion that happiness has not increased over the past one hundred years, noticing that the wording of the question has changed over the decades. For example, in Japan in the late 1950s and early '60s, the most positive answer the pollsters offered was, "Although I am not innumerably satisfied, I am generally satisfied with life now." In 1964, the most positive answer became "Completely satisfied," which is quite different. If you adjust the time series for the way the question is worded, they found that happiness in Europe and Japan has significantly increased. Easterlin responded (2010) and maintained his original views, and even Wolfers and Stevenson still conceded that in the United States, Korea, and China, happiness has not trended upward over the past thirty-five years, a rather large portion of the data.

This type of dispute is typical of every fact mentioned in this book. If you look at different countries at different times holding various other variables constant, you can get different results. This why taking a view of the broader scope of data and then looking at the best underlying narrative is so important, because the data are never definitive within one case, regardless of the power of the statistical technique. The evidence is compelling, in my opinion, because it is so broad.

6.3 Politics of Envy

As Hayek noted in *The Use of Knowledge in Society*, an individualist society decentralizes decision making and gives a profit incentive to those with the ability to know important facts about economizing on means versus ends. It is clear from extreme examples such East and West Germany and North and South Korea that individualism is more efficient than the more materially egalitarian socialist economies. Yet as the classicist Moses Finley liked to say, all revolutionary movements had a single program, "cancel the debts and redistribute the land," the ultimate economic equalizer.[128] There's a constant tension inherent in society driven by libertarian and egalitarian instincts that have evolved throughout human history.

Anthropologist Christopher Boehm at UCLA notes that dominance hierarchies are a defining characteristic of every known civilization before modern times and are characteristic of all nonhuman hominid societies, such as the alpha male silverback gorilla lording it over his band of mates. It is a curious fact that dominance hierarchies are rare in the ethnographic literature describing hunting-and-gathering societies—and thus, presumably, also rare in hunting-and-gathering societies as they existed during much of our common evolutionary past.

To account for this fact, Boehm proposed the idea of a reverse dominance hierarchy. The gist of his idea is that while standard alpha male dominance was common to the human species during our long, shared hominid past, we developed an innate distaste of being dominated by others. Armed with a motive and using the cooperative skills that language and their big brains conferred upon them, all the lesser males in a group who were in danger of being dominated by an alpha male would form a reverse dominance hierarchy to put the would-be tyrant in his place. In this way, dominance behavior, though not eliminated, could be moderated and dispersed. Unlike gorillas, humans can do things such as get up in the middle of the night and use a spear to dispatch the most physically intimidating person quite easily—all it takes is motive and a little conspiracy. Leaders generally maintain their positions not by dominating but by consolidating majority opinion.

Certainly in modern society people care about their relative status, which paradoxically breeds a desire for egalitarian results. As anthropologist Harold Schneider put it, "All men seek to rule, but if they cannot, they seek to be equal." Upstarts are put in their place in a variety of ways. For example, !Kung bushmen will mock the gift of someone because they see gift giving as an attempt to signal superior status.[129] In effect, they ridicule this act because they see it as a pretext for signaling dominance. In more complex hunter-gatherer societies, groups of men will actually kill an upstart for a crime conveniently determined.[130]

Politics is fundamentally about redistribution and efficiency, usually with the latter a pretext for the former because no one is against efficiency. The economic disparity between various groups hits at our egalitarian instincts, and motivates many legislative priorities. The focus on outcomes and not rights is based on the idea that the market is generally a rigged game, and people become unequal mainly through forces beyond their control (e.g., institutional discrimination, parents). As a libertarian, I think this premise is factually incorrect, and regardless top-down directives are generally even less fair for reasons outlined by Friedrich Hayek among others. Yet, I empathize with those who focus on relative rather than absolute condition because it is based on a fundamental instinct.

6.4 Benchmarking

Many people are bored by talk of utility and philosophy but readily understand benchmarking. In equity mutual funds, the practice is taken as a given—the top funds are generally given top honors in annual reviews. It takes for granted that the mean return is taken out because everyone knows that the general market direction is not in their mandate mainly because it became painfully obvious that adding market timing to stock selection was an inferior strategy. In the index next to "Risk" in fund manager Kenneth Fisher's book *Only Three Questions That Count*, it merely says, "See Benchmarking." Indeed, it *does* make practical sense to benchmark, which is why it is so common, but this only highlights my point: if everyone is benchmarking, the result is no general risk premium, and, further, that low-returning lottery tickets are still held by the masses within their index and closet-index funds.

Consider CAPM founding father and Nobel Laureate Bill Sharpe. He consults for pension funds evaluating asset managers and states his first objective: "I want a product to be defined relative to a benchmark."[131] In an interview, Paul Samuelson stated, "You know that happiness is having a little more money than your colleagues." As mentioned in the introduction, when asked about the nature of risk in small stocks, Eugene Fama noted that in the 1980s, "small stocks were in a depression," and Merton Miller noted the underperformance of the Dimensional Fund Advisors small-cap portfolio against the S&P 500 for six years in a row was evidence of its risk.[132] Small stocks actually had higher returns relative to the risk-free rate in the 1980s compared to the 1970s, so why was this considered a depression? Because they lagged their benchmark, the S&P 500, which went up even more.

Harry Markowitz told the story that when he went to apply his theory on the efficient frontier that really started modern portfolio theory to his personal portfolio back in the 1960s, he simply split his portfolio 50–50 between bonds and stocks because "I visualized my grief if the stock market went way up and I wasn't in it—or if it went way down and I was completely in it." In an interview in 2005, Markowitz said, "Let's look back at the last bubble—the tech bubble. People would look around and see other people making money much faster than they were, so they decided they would imitate them—a natural thing."[133]

In other words, all the key academics who developed the standard model act as if they were maximizing a relative status utility function, not the one holding up their seminal papers. It seems reasonable to presume that for these investment professionals and academics, risk, intuitively, is a return relative to a benchmark. If all investors act as if they were benchmarking to aggregate indexes, risk is not priced in equilibrium.

6.5 Virtue Always in Moderation

Risk taking is synonymous with the virtue of courage. Courage is the most universally admired virtue because it is the hardest, by definition, doing something we are afraid to do. Most courage is not related to physical courage today because warfare and violence have decreased so much relative to classical times, but courage is even more needed intellectually when we reject the opinions of others. Often this puts one in the position of being a crank, like those who think the moon landings were faked, but other times we have heroes like Nikolai

Tesla, who fought the famous Thomas Edison advocating the more efficient alternating over direct current. A crank is simply someone with a minority opinion among his peers, and the key to whether that person is considered a genius or stupid is whether he was correct, which is often known only with hindsight. The courage we generally face is the courage to risk humiliation, to believe differently than everyone else, deviate from the consensus. This is related to a mutual fund managers' benchmark risk.

Virtues are things that we think make us more successful in life. Their positive effects are not shortcuts to success but hit at the core of what makes people appreciated now and forever. The four classic virtues are temperance, prudence, courage, and justice, though one could expand the list to include politeness, fidelity, justice, generosity, compassion, mercy, gratitude, humility, simplicity, tolerance, purity, gentleness, good faith, and humor. A lot of this gets down to semantics, as the Roman Stoic Seneca argued that all virtues are the result of prudence.

Most of us believe we are virtuous because we all wish to be doing that which is best for ourselves, and virtues are by definition helpful. Even a thief can think he is merely serving a greater good, flouting one rule for a higher one, such as giving vigor to an otherwise flaccid society. Aristotle defined a virtue as a balance point between a deficiency and an excess of a trait.[134] The point of greatest virtue lies not in the exact middle but somewhere in between two extremes: moderation in all things.

Tolerance is a virtue, but too much tolerance can show a lack of integrity or courage. Politeness is a virtue and includes not taking offense at unintentional slights, but if you really think someone's behavior is wrong even though unintentional, not taking offense could imply you just don't care enough to correct that person's ways; you can be too polite to be honest and vice versa.[135] And so it goes for all the virtues. There is no virtue that can be applied unthinkingly because different virtues conflict at extreme points, which is why Plato stated that virtues cannot exist independently but rather like the ingredients that make a cake: all in the right amounts.[136]

Risk taking and the courage it implies generates a risk premium in the standard model that is strictly linear; all standard models generate this result. If you take more risk, it adds to your wealth over time, the first bit as much as the last. There is no sense of context, or objective excess. If the returns to such courage were of this form, it would be an anomaly to the payoffs of every other virtue.

Consider education, which most people think increases one's human capital. There does appear to be a large wage premium differential for college graduates—about 80 percent—though it is unclear whether this reflects signaling or true increases in value. Nevertheless, this income correlation breaks down at higher levels, where PhDs involve another five years work without much increase in earnings compared to stopping at a bachelor's degree. It also varies considerably by major, as a Peace Studies major is not going to generate the same average college premium as a chemistry major. Education is correlated with income but there's clearly no linear relationship here.

Risk taking is good as the optimum between cowardice and recklessness, but in between is where it gets tricky. To say it's all a fair trade, from the first penny to the last, trivializes the process, making it much less important and less anxiety producing than it is. Risks we incur must be appropriate to the ends we seek. Consider anger. Aristotle noted that being angry was easy, "but to be angry with the right person and to the right degree and at the right time and for the right purpose, and in the right way", is not easy. That is a lot of context, but it is also true, highlighting how difficult it is to apply any behavioral tactic.

An example of how a virtue as an explanation wealth can be wrong is the premium to courage that supposedly explained the natural position of the aristocracy. It is quaint, but in centuries past, there were titled classes who thought they deserved to have higher status independent of their work or intelligence. They did not think it was totally unearned because nobility was based on courage.

Classical liberal Richard Cobden wrote, "The battle-plain is the harvest-field of the aristocracy, watered by the blood of the people," meaning the aristocracy prior to 1900 generated their legitimacy via their willingness to lead groups into battle, often needlessly. As the British aristocracy declined from 1880 to 1910, they thought that World War I would reestablish them as the top of their country. Many were eager to fight; their primary fear circa 1914 was that the fighting would be over before they could prove themselves in battle. While they subsequently lost proportionately more of their sons than those of other classes in WW I, the decline of the aristocracy continued unabated after the Great War. Indeed, the loss of life sharply curtailed the supply of domestic servants, and inheritance taxes went from nothing to 60 percent by 1939. The lower classes felt no sense of gratitude toward the aristocracy, having lost enough themselves. Battlefield courage is admirable, but it is not sufficiently rare to generate privileged status; the lower classes were not party to such an exchange.

In retrospect, the aristocracy arrogated power via myth, tradition, and brute force rationalized via their bloodline's exceptional courage. The problem with their self-serving story is that many would accept a probability of death for such success, so this "courage premium" was not a real equilibrium result, as WW I showed. Courage was a necessary, not sufficient, condition for acquiring power. Similarly, risk taking is a necessary condition to achieving riches, but that does not logically imply a positive general relation. In standard financial theory, if you take risk, on average you will get rich quicker than others, a statistically sufficient condition. A lot of people would be willing to put their funds in some blind, risky trust at a young age if they knew that this were the objectively superior highest expected return at retirement. Indeed, this is the argument in Jeremy Siegel's book *Stocks for the Long Run*, that over a generation the probability that stocks underperform bonds is extremely low.[137]

There is no simple form of risk taking such that, if you can tie yourself to some intellectual mast and bear this psychic pain you should expect a higher return. A lot of our bad intuitions arise from bad analogies, and here the analogy is that because risk taking at some level has a positive return, it generalizes to any level of risk taking.

Mindless exposure to volatility of any sort—idiosyncratic, systematic, total—is a sure path to financial oblivion. Consider that professional athletes are both wealthy and risk takers. They have high levels of testosterone, which is correlated with higher-than-average financial risk taking.[138] In the standard line of reasoning, irrational investors who take too much risk have higher expected returns because their miscalibration increases their exposure to the higher returning assets.[139] Yet being not so bright is a cancer on your wealth because all sorts of people are trying to separate less intelligent people from whatever money they have. The *New York Times* estimated that 60 percent of NBA players are broke only five years after retirement, even though the average salary was $5.85M in 2009.[140] If mere risk preferences were sufficient, they should have above-average returns, but in reality their poor returns are what happens when risk taking is combined with a lack of prudence.[141]

Shane Frederick found that a short g-loaded test is highly correlated with a subject's preference for higher expected value choices.[142] That is, framed probabilistically, the lower the cognitive score, the greater the chance of not accurately framing expected values. This suggests less intelligent people will make more analytic mistakes, which seems tautological. As an anecdote of my thesis, I could not do better than the study by Grinblatt et al. (2011), which looked at a great set of Finnish data, and because all Finns have to serve in their army, the data gathered a rather unbiased set of data on IQs and later wealth characteristics. They found that IQ was positively correlated with equity market participation, and higher IQ investors tended to be more diversified with lower beta stocks. Thus the low IQ investors appear to be rationally avoiding the market because when they do invest, they do so very inefficiently, and I suspect they do worse in avoiding the high transaction cost strategies and tactics. The inefficient investing that generates so much fee income to the financial community depends on naiveté, ignorance, or laziness, and these investors generate a predictable footprint.[143]

If risk were the mere pain of loss, the same pain experienced by others, it would be a lot like exposing oneself to working in smelly occupations. Yet septic tank work does not pay well, and the untouchables in India have long had a monopoly on cleaning sewers manually without much compensation; people get used to a lot of things. In a similar way, risk taking, if all it takes is a willingness to expose oneself to some stochastic shocks, is too easy. As Dan Pink noted, researchers have documented that monetary incentives work pretty easily for straightforward mechanical tasks such as keeping one's hand in hot water for extended periods, while monetary incentives tend to not work well for creative goals.[144] In a similar way, if mere willingness to undergo stochastic shocks generates higher expected returns, it would be too easy, as people will tolerate anything nonlethal for a steady income. Society does not pay people *merely* for exposing themselves to bad things such as death, smelliness, or portfolio volatility. Just like all the other virtues, risk must be pursued with moderation and prudence applied to the trade-offs with other virtues.

6.6 Conclusion

The risk premium is directly linked to the standard utility function; they exist in an "if and only if" condition where one implies the other and vice versa. If we do not see risk premiums in general, rather than piecemeal explanations a more parsimonious solution is to change this fundamental assumption. The movement from greed to envy or from absolute to relative wealth can get you there. Economists have become comfortable with simple self-interest, the idea that people are interested solely in their own wealth accumulation, because they discovered it was actually benign, if not altruistic.

The move from looking at absolute wealth to relative wealth is important, and only the relative wealth assumption is consistent with a missing risk premium. Relative utility seems more evolutionarily robust, more consistent with what makes us happy, more consistent with ubiquitous benchmarking, and more consistent with research from neuroscience, ethology, anthropology, and psychology. The standard utility function, with its implication of a linear reward function, would be unprecedented within the context of all our other virtues.

CHAPTER 7

Why We Take Too Much Financial Risk

If risk taking did not pay off, presumably no one would do it because, by definition, risk is something we do not like. Risk taking, however, is unavoidable, and it does pay off, just not in the way implied by the standard model, where incremental amounts of risk taking, which is the same for everyone, pays off.

Consider the optimal stopping problem, which has an extensive literature in the fields of applied probability, statistics, and decision theory.[145] Assume you are looking to get married and have kids, and your lifetime and fertility are finite. You can go out on a dates with willing partners to assess their quality, but once you reject them, you can no longer contact them. You do not know the exact quality distribution of willing partners, you see only a sequence of candidates when you sample them. A date is costly and time consuming. The question is about the optimal strategy (stopping rule) to maximize the probability of selecting the best mate, given you are uncertain of how good a mate you can get and you have a finite life.

The mathematics generates results such as you go on thirty-one dates and then choose the first person better than any of that sample you first met. Choosing a real career or mate has many other dimensions that make such a simple rule incomplete, but the logic remains: for any choice you make will probably be suboptimal compared to if you had perfect information; your choice relative to the optimal choice seen by an omniscient deity is invariably inferior. Both choosing to move on or staying with what you have involves risk; risk cannot be avoided. We all took risks when we rejected and then selected mates, careers, and other important things, often at ages when we were quite ignorant, because life is short.[146] In this way, we are all familiar with the benefits and pitfalls of taking risk.

Psychologist Roy Baumeister made an interesting observation. He noted that, historically, 80 percent of females have reproduced, but only 40 percent of males have passed on their genes. The rest of the males have been genetic dead ends.[147] Historically, a female could play it safe because there were always men willing to impregnate them, whereas a male who remained meek was elbowed out of sexual trysts. Males have to beat out other males to get access to females. Thus men built ships and traveled to far-off lands because those were the guys who had more children, whereas a bunch of women could bear children just as easily staying put. Everyone's male ancestors have been disproportionately risk takers; not taking risk, over generations, is certain doom. We take risks, therefore, because not taking risk is genetic suicide, at least for the gender that generally takes such risks.

Risk takers dominate our lives via their disproportionate effect on our genes and their influence on our technology and culture. They did not become successful, however, merely by taking some abstract risk that is the same for everyone and then enjoy the higher rewards that came with it. They instead took the right risks, those consistent with their unique strengths, and reaped rewards consistent with a mastery of something important. For example, a headlock is generally a bad wrestling move, but if you have a good headlock and your opponent is leaning into you, it can be very effective at any level. That is, a high expected return decision is a function of context and comparative advantage, not a covariance.

One might say this is not relevant to markets where rational traders at the margin determine prices and returns. This is misleading for two reasons. First, while it is difficult to find strategies that generate Sharpes greater than one because of rational traders affecting prices, improving a Sharpe by 0.2 is possible precisely because stupid investors do influence equilibrium prices though this opportunity is not large enough to invite arbitrage. Secondly, given the multidimensional complexity of any asset class, where different trading tactics and complementary positions generate very different returns, the same asset class has very different net returns depending on the investor; I know people who do quite well investing in options, and I also know that most people waste a lot of money in that area.

The economist Robert Aumann discussed the difference between rule and act optimality and gave the following example.[148] In the ultimatum game two players interact to decide how to divide a sum of money given to them. So the first player is given $100, and then proposes the second player receive some fraction, say $30 (first player then receiving $70). If the second player rejects, neither player receives anything. If the second player accepts, the money is split according to the proposal. The game is played only once and anonymously, so that reciprocation is not an issue.

Most people reject an offer less than 20 percent of the pool. Economists see this as irrational because there is no upside to rejecting the money in this game, but Aumann sees it as rational in the general sense that one does not want to appear a chump, even if the appearance is just to oneself. The chump rule overrides our act rationality because humans have evolved to follow rules, as it is simply too costly to go through life without such heuristics.[149] It is costly to be always thinking out optimal strategies and very useful to have simple time-saving instincts and snap judgments. Our brains are only so big; our narrative self can really handle only one problem at any one time, so rules of thumb are useful heuristics.

People have an intuitive rule that risk taking is good. However, the idea that because taking risk is valuable, essential, and unavoidable in one's life, in finding one's career or soul mate, this does not imply that risk begets a higher expected return for everyone in every time and place (risk properly measured, of course). People should see risk taking as a process of self-discovery, becoming the best you can in that which you are best suited. The payoffs to risk taking are partially chance, but if you want to take risks intelligently, you gravitate toward risks consistent with your skills and get better and better at them. If some risk taking demands nothing of you other than willingness, it is surely foolhardy because such willingness is hardly in short supply, so these types of risks do not generate higher-than-average-returns as a general rule.

7.1 Investors Ignoring the Standard Theory

In the standard model, choices are ex ante optimal and there's no anxiety. While ex post we may regret the choice, a rational person knows that such choices are made in the face of randomness, so the outcome *per se* should not affect whether this was a good choice ex ante. Textbook investment choices are usually completely defined and reducible to simple logic.

Economists are very good at analyzing objective uncertainty, where the complete model, including the exact stochastic process, is known as well as anyone can know it. In these situations, people generally act as modeled. [150] Yet it is precisely because real risk taking is quite different, making different decisions than the consensus based on a radically different interpretation of the objective odds implicit in the investment, that we experience anxiety. In practice, financial risk taking involves a great deal of anxiety, not about the realization of objective odds but rather sensing whether or not one has correctly ascertained the correct odds, what is called "ambiguity aversion." [151] Real-world data show an array of connections between events that are impossible to fully see in finite time. [152]

Classic investors like J.P. Morgan and Benjamin Graham distinguished between gambling and investing, the former being simple exposure to randomness, the latter something amenable to special insight and intuition. A good investment has the odds decidedly stacked in its favor via some special insight. Most investors feel they take risks this way, even if most are objectively wrong.

Economists have long known the behavioral implications of the CAPM were incorrect. Investors are underdiversified, with one study showing that 25 percent of investors have only one stock, and more than 50 percent owned fewer than three stocks. [153] Their risk taking is clearly far different from that presumed in the CAPM framework which focuses on systematic risk (i.e., beta). Furthermore, consider that brokerages recommend only stocks with above-average returns. [154] If the standard model is correct, as half of all stocks have below-average expected returns, then such stocks merely have lower-than-average risk. Half of all stocks have this characteristic, supposedly, yet absolutely zero show up as recommendations, a rather stark absence. If we go outside of brokerages, the bizarre Internet investment schemes all have one common characteristic: they promise greater-than-average returns. With relative utility and the zero-risk premium, this makes sense; with standard utility, this makes no sense.

An example of this bias is Dimensional Fund Advisors, which is a creation of an all-star cast of academics associated with the current standard model. It was created based on the finding that small-cap stocks generated above average returns. [155] Now, according to standard theory, a higher return is merely a trade-off for the higher risk of such a portfolio. Nonetheless, like everyone else in a relative status economy, the only thing that motivates an investment deviation from the benchmark status quo is a higher-than-average return. Dimensional initially ignored the lower-than-average returning large-cap stocks that presumably were just as attractive in their paradigm.

Similarly, Campbell Harvey, former editor of the *Journal of Finance* and an embodiment of conventional wisdom about risk and returns, also discovered some technical rules for generating above-average returns within commodity futures, and noted they were "attractive."[156] Looking at momentum and the contract forward curve, he found a way to generate "above average returns." Of course, such higher returns are more attractive as a practical matter, but theoretically—in the standard model—they are associated with higher risk, no more desirable than those assets with lower expected returns (and thus less risky). In practice, no one, not even the high priests of this view, act as if their theory were true whenever they discover a higher-than-average returning strategy.

People take risk by not merely turning dials everyone understands to a higher set point but rather doing things that generate above average returns because of perceived systematic errors made by the masses. Of course such person could be making an error himself, which is why these choices produce anxiety; such a failure would have implications beyond any one decision. The key, however, is that when people take risk, they are generally not doing it *more* but rather, *differently*.[157]

As mentioned in section 5.4, a relative status utility function implies people will not completely arbitrage overbought conditions. The relative risk from deviating from the benchmark market portfolio implies that any asset with abnormal demand will have lower-than-average returns. Yet it remains to be explained why people are so predisposed to buy highly risky assets, those lottery tickets with the highest payouts and lowest average returns, because it is not a rational expected return. Below are the several reasons that could explain this preference for highly risky assets.

7.2 Winner's Curse

The "wisdom of crowds" applies to the means, so that average guesses of the weight of an ox, estimated future inflation rate or the number of jelly beans in a jar are going to be pretty close to the true number because people's errors tend to be randomly distributed high and low. But if average is good, then necessarily the top guesses are biased upward. In the 1950s, they came up with the term "winner's curse" to describe the fact that for auctions of offshore oil fields, winners were generally cursed by winning. Consider a field that had an actual value of $10 million, and that oil companies might guess its value to be anywhere from $5 million to $20 million. The winner is the bidder making the highest estimate. If we assume that the average bid is accurate, then the highest bidder overestimates the item's value. Thus the auction's winner is likely to overpay.

A more sophisticated bidder would shade his bid based on the number of other bidders and the perceived distribution of their valuation. This is not straightforward because even though the number of bidders may be estimated fairly easily, their valuation distributions are much less objective. Nonetheless, overpaying via a winner's curse is not a rational equilibrium.

In 1977, Edward Miller presented a model where investors with different opinions were buying assets. He noted that in such a case, an asset with a greater dispersion of opinion would have higher prices, given the same average expected return. If there are constraints on short selling, which as a practical matter there are, the extreme buyers are not counterweighted by extreme shorts. Consider if one hundred investors were looking at buying a stock and there were only shares enough to satisfy five investors, and there is no short selling. The greater the dispersion of valuations, the greater the 95th percentile valuation given a constant mean; meaning, the clearing price for the stock would be higher the higher the dispersion of valuations if you assumed no short selling.

Over time, Miller's winner's curse argument has become more popular for several reasons. First, the data on low-returning/high-risk assets have grown in many areas, so it is no longer a disputed fact (e.g., in IPOs or cross-sectionally for equities).[158] Work on analyst expectation dispersion naturally lends itself to this kind of analysis, especially when the dispersion is correlated with lower returns, as predicted by Miller.[159] Lastly, the popularity of *Freakonomics* and behavioralism in the 1990s lent credence to 'partial equilibrium' results that were previously considered implausible because they implied arbitrage (in general one can short sell).

Interestingly, Ed Miller was the first to emphasize the efficacy of low-beta investing in a *Journal of Portfolio Management* article in 2001, noting that if the winner's curse was responsible for the poor performance of high-beta stocks; the risk-reward ratio for low-beta stocks was obviously higher.[160] Though others may have noted the low return to high volatility stocks, Miller was the first to really have a theory as to why this was the essence to their returns, not merely an incidental feature. The key is that one needs to believe in a theory to really think a pattern isn't measurement error but rather some kind of opportunity, and the winner's curse applied to stocks was his original idea and allowed him to identify the low-volatility opportunity before anyone else in an academic journal.

The effects of the winner's curse or any of the following theories that lead to higher demand for volatile assets all need some sort of constraint in the standard model to prevent rational agents from making these effects imperceptible in equilibrium. Thus for the winner's curse or any of these biases toward high volatility to be relevant in the standard model, we need both irrational buyers who do not foresee their buying bias and a general equilibrium effect that keeps outsiders from shorting these markets, predictably anticipating the overoptimistic dupes. With relative utility an extra demand by one set of investors will not generate offsetting arbitrage by their investing complement, and no such ad hoc constraints are needed.

7.3 Overconfidence

Perhaps the most celebrated overconfidence anecdote is Svenson's (1981) finding that 93 percent of American drivers rate themselves as better than the median.[161] There are plenty of other such findings, and they do not relate only to the uneducated: 94 percent of college professors think they are above-average teachers; 90 percent of entrepreneurs think that their new business will be a success; 98 percent of students who take the SAT say they have average or above-average leadership skills.[162] Barber and Odean (1999) used overconfidence to explain why men, who psychological studies show are more overconfident than women, trade too much.

On nearly any dimension that is both subjective and socially desirable, most people see themselves as better than average. People who think they are better than average at stock picking or picking mutual funds, will necessarily focus on the highly volatile stocks that generate better rewards for their prescience: why waste time on stocks that at best will outperform by 20 percent when another could outperform by 80 percent? Highly volatile assets attract overconfident investors.

Given this effect is so prevalent, it is useful to see why overconfidence can be helpful. Robert Trivers argued that we continually paint a distorted picture of the world so that we might more easily get our way with others.[163] You are a better liar to others if you first lie to yourself because then you generate fewer unconscious signals that liars make in gestures and intonation. This involves constantly inflating our achievements and abilities and rationalizing our mistakes. For example, he noted that children not only lie, but lie more the higher their IQ. When presented with pictures that are manipulated to make people look better than they are, people's brain's light up via fMRI, recognizing the self that is 20 percent better looking than the real thing. That is, we truly see ourselves as better looking than we are (notably, only by a plausible amount).

Beyond the simple manipulation of others, the results back up the benefits of being a little overoptimistic, as people who hold positive illusions about themselves, their abilities, and their future prospects are mentally healthier, happier, and better liked than people who lack such illusion. They have lower rates of mortality and a variety of health benefits.[164] People who are confident about the future continue trying, even when it's hard. People like optimistic people because they tend to be less defensive, less easy to offend, and are more likely to assume the good faith of others. Economist and Psychologist Danny Kahneman states this is the one bias he most wants his children to have because of its myriad benefits.[165]

The human brain has difficulty generating rational intuition for situations that did not exist in ancestral environments, what psychologist Satoshi Kanazaw calls the 'Savanna principle.'[166] Thus it is not surprising that this generally salubrious bias, optimism, is counterproductive in the evolutionarily novel human activity of investing financial wealth, were excessive confidence leads to folly.

7.4 Risk-Loving Preferences

Friedman and Savage (1948) were the first to really apply utility functions to financial decision making, and, interestingly, it was not the concept risk aversion that they concentrated upon but rather the paradox that people liked to gamble *and* buy insurance. This inflected utility function has a portion below that is risk loving—you prefer uncertainty to a sure thing—and above some point where one is risk averse. Such a utility function is also present in Kahneman and Tversky's prospect theory, which was reinvigorated by Kahneman's 2003 Nobel Prize. Thus we have some portion of our utility where we are risk loving (the convex portions) and some where we are risk averse (the concave portions).

FIGURE 7.1. *An inflected utility function*

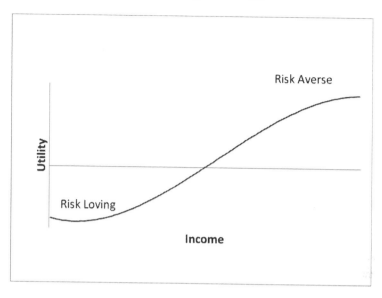

Consider that one of prospect theory's key implications is that our aversion to losses is much stronger than our enjoyment of gains: the basic frame for our utility functions is at our current wealth, whatever that is. On its face, this suggests not so much risk loving but loss hating, as losses are disliked much more than gains are liked. This makes people willing to pay for insurance to avoid big losses, and also why they gamble, because they overweight the small probabilities of winning large amounts. In this framework these are not probability errors, but rather subjective weightings.[167]

Risk loving shows up in the literature on skewness preference, where investors presumably pay a premium for assets with right (up) payoff skewness. Investors should prefer assets with large upward skews.[168] Post, Levy, and van Vliet (2002) noted that if one adds the condition that investors are still globally risk averse, which all these skew-loving papers also presume, the skewness preference should be only a fraction—around 15 percent—of the theoretical premium to "the risky market." Instead, most researchers who look at this find skewness risk premiums of around 3 percent, which is inconsistent with any purported market risk premiums of around 5 percent. Now, I think the market risk premium of 5 percent is empirically wrong, but the point here is consistency, that in their frameworks these are not compatible results. If a skewness risk premium is 2 percent, the market risk premium must be implausibly high, around 15 percent.[169]

Risk loving and overconfidence are difficult to distinguish in practice, as they both would explain why people prefer highly volatile assets. Justin Wolfers and Erik Snowberg published a paper that could distinguish between these two hypotheses.[170] They did this by looking at horse racing returns to single horses and for combinations such as the exacta where one chooses the first and second horses in a race. The theories imply different relative odds for the combinations and the underlying single horse races.[171] For example, an exacta is a bet on which horse will place first and which will place second. A risk-loving model can be constructed to explain the pricing of simple bets on the winners, but these lead to inaccurate implications for pricing of the exacta bets, whereas the miscalibration model fits the exacta pricing. In sum, they find that racetrack betters are overconfident, not risk lovers. Thus, I find the risk-loving story for why people are drawn to highly risky stocks dominated by the similar-looking 'overconfidence' story.

7.5 Information Costs

Stocks with higher volatility generate more news than less volatile firms. Such stocks are then in play and so become relevant to the investor interested in deviating from the index. Stocks that are in the news generate lots of information that fiduciaries can use to sell their ideas to clients. Such cocktail party stories are very helpful, and it is much easier to talk about something in the news than something where everyone is fairly ignorant, save for some objective value metrics.

In my 1996 *Journal of Finance* paper on mutual fund preferences, I found that volatility was positively correlated with the relative ownership percentage of mutual funds in regressions that included price, size, and other characteristics.[172] A simple reason for this institutional preference could be it is easy to form an opinion on companies that are moving around, generating lots of commentary and analysis. Indeed, I also documented that in the context of these other variables. Stocks more frequently in the news that had been around longer tended to have larger mutual fund ownership. One could imagine funds being both more aware of these companies and having an easier time explaining their ownership in these companies.

A study by Arthur J. O'Connor at Pace University documented a strong correlation between things like the number of Facebook fans, Twitter followers, YouTube views, and contemporaneous stock price, looking at thirty highly recognized brands.[173] It seems reasonable that one explanation of the correlation is that the more people hear about a company, the more it gets considered as an investment.

7.6 Alpha Discovery

Objective tests serve two purposes: to inform the test taker and those observing him. To outsiders, this is signaling and serves as useful information as to whether this person should be entrusted with greater financial responsibility, but the agent himself may have uncertainty that needs resolving via objective tests. In either case, the mechanism is the same, to see if an investor is able to generate a superior return. That is, does she have alpha?

Many people believe they have an ability to pick stocks successfully. To demonstrate this ability, they have to actually pick stocks and document the results. It may all be luck, but if people believe that their short-run performance signals alpha, that information would be considered valuable regardless. This biases investors toward the more volatile assets so they can assess their investing alpha more clearly, expediting the process.

Many people trade as if they might have alpha. In such a scenario, the quickest way to discern alpha is by buying volatile stocks, ones that clearly signal success, because learning one's type early here is valuable.

7.7 Representativeness Bias

This is a classic bias from the classic book on biases, Kahneman, Tversky, and Slovac (1984). The idea is base rate information is neglected in a Bayesian sense relative to the ease to which some anecdotes are recalled. When one thinks of great investments, they think of companies that were highly speculative at one time, such as Microsoft or Apple. Almost by definition, any stock that rose tenfold was highly volatile over much of its meteoric rise. This is implied in the saying, "To get rich, you have to take risk." Yet the converse does not logically hold, mainly that taking risk makes you rich, even statistically. Think of the idea that to win the lottery, you have to buy a ticket, but buying a ticket will not make you rich on average.

The problem with this thinking is that one needs to find all the stocks that were like Apple in 1977 or Microsoft in 1986, and when we do this, such stocks tend to perform poorly. Some do very well, but they are anomalies. Thus our inference from success is necessarily biased toward riskiness paying off, but this is just a look-back bias from assuming those cases easiest to recall are most representative. Interestingly, many successful people, such as Steve Jobs and Bill

Gates, both of whom dropped out of college, also contain this bias. Certainly few would recommend to young students they drop out of college because this is what many successful entrepreneurs did because we know that on average this is not a good strategy.

People under the presumption that risky assets are in the class of assets that makes people rich are operating under this bias. Highly volatile stocks dominate our conception of great stock investments when looked at anecdotally, though as a class they fail miserably. Highly successful investments are disproportionately risky, but this trait does not represent an expected return factor.

7.8 Convex Payoffs to Professionals

The flow of investor funds is a highly convex function of fund performance: really high for the top decile but then evening out to almost indifference below the 50th percentile, rather like a call option.[174] The pattern applies to raw returns without any risk adjustment; investors are suckers for the biggest winners in the latest bull market. Just as in a call option valuation, the higher the variance of the underlying performance, the greater the value to the investment fund. Funds are responding to a signal, but the point here is simply to acknowledge this investor response as a fact and note the fund behavior it encourages. Regardless of the rationality of investor behavior, the fact remains that customer fund flows as they exist encourage fund complexes to take risks that increase their chances of being in top ten lists at the end of the year, which clearly encourages risk taking.

The nature of this call-option type mechanism is highlighted by the standard nature of quarterly and annual reviews of portfolio managers. Generally, a top ten list is created based solely on returns. Morningstar assigns a ranking from one to five stars based on the total return normalized by the equity category minus a risk metric based on the number of months with drawdown, but this too is heavily dominated by the mere return. *Bloomberg Magazine* actually highlights analysts by their most profitable picks, where highlighted analysts have returns around 100 percent on various picks; and you simply can't make such articles without taking a large gamble.[175]

7.9 Conclusion

Rational investors should identify and short risky, low returning stocks in the standard model. Thus short constraints, and the premise that the entire ownership base (including index funds) is irrational, are necessary conditions for the exogenous risky demand to cause lower-than-average returns for risky assets in the standard model. In a relative status model, this kind of extreme additional assumption is not needed, because shorting or avoiding these risky assets exposes one to more benchmark risk.

Those uncertain choices we make with incomplete information are not confined to finance, and indeed surveys show that the most prominent regrets in people's lives are not portfolio choices but choices about careers, romance, and parenting.[176] Thus we all have intuition as to how to take risks because we all take them. Unfortunately, this life-enhancing rule that taking risk is essential and important leads to intuition that supports the standard theory, that risk taking properly defined increases one's expected returns without context.

There are several reasons the masses are drawn to volatile assets like a moth to a flame, but these effects must be paired with a relative utility argument, or ad hoc constraints. Only in a relative utility framework will those not affected by this volatility attraction not seek to counter the effect via eliminating such assets from their benchmarks or shorting them.

CHAPTER 8

Why This Bad Theory Is So Popular

I believe one of the fundamental assumptions of asset pricing is incorrect, basically that if you replace greed with envy, you explain more data. Currently most professors disagree with this interpretation of the facts. They would say that perhaps within some markets at some times there is a flat or even negative 'risk' premium, and correspondingly that a relative status utility function is relevant only to these special cases. I think these reservations will slowly fade away because a correct theory's best friend is time. I have watched my argument described as unimportant, trivial, wrong, obvious, and even illegal, but the trend is clearly positive, as evidenced by the now common acceptance of the fact that low-volatility stocks outperform the basic indices.[177]

Douglas Hofstadter once said, "'for every debate in science there is an isomorphic debate in the methodology of science.'"[178] Therefore I think it's useful to outline why academics have been so slow to adjust their failed paradigm, why they are not embracing what I see as an obvious corrective to an empirically vacuous theory.

8.1 Moralistic Fallacy

The main reason academics really like their standard conception of utility is that it is so useful to modelers, and economists are primarily modelers. While the naturalistic fallacy presumes that nature is what ought to be, the moralistic fallacy is the reverse: what ought to be, is. If everyone's utility is relative, it is difficult to talk about what societies should do. Economics loses a lot of its ability to objectively determine what to do in this scenario. The concept of a better outcome using the weak Pareto criterion, where at least one person is better off and no one is worse off, simply is not relevant because everyone's relative gain in any change comes from someone else's relative loss. Previously, if you thought that you could reify the economy in one person, then the wealthier an economy becomes, the happier everyone is. With relative utility, aggregate wealth has no obvious implication for general welfare.[179]

The assumption of individual optimizers was initially seen as a cynical assumption, but Adam Smith and Friedrich Hayek highlighted how such narrow self interest can aggregate to counterintuitive socially beneficial outcomes[180] Later, game theorists such as Robert Axelrod and evolutionary biologists such as Robert Trivers showed that altruism is consistent with self-interest in repeated interactions.[181] The assumptions seemed evolutionarily stable, prosocial, and allowed highly abstract model to generate insights with unambiguous outcomes. Ought and is, positive and normative, are often in accord in the standard approach where people are indifferent of others.

A modeler is good at taking assumptions and rigorously deriving inevitable truths, and as economists aspire to be scientists, mastery of this method is what defines the dominant academic economists of the past 50 years. These models have much more obvious implications and interesting equilibria if the standard utility functions are true. If individual utility were dependent of others, economic models would be a lot less tractable, a lot more ambiguous. Given the actual irrelevance of economic theory to most pressing economic debates, the current paradigm seems based more on wishful thinking than any empirical success.

8.2 Wrong for a Long Time

Phlogiston, aether, Skinner's behaviorism, psychoanalysis, and Marxism are all wrong, but only the physical theories have been abandoned because you can never conclusively disprove a social theory. Thus theoretical pioneers generally go to their graves thinking they have discovered a profound truth, one that perhaps has been empirically troubled, confused by malicious critics or superficial anomalies but ultimately like the theory of germs or atoms, something that will revolutionize our conception of reality.

In finance, the initial idea was that risk measured via a correlation with the market would show a risk premium. Now it is risk with something like the market return, something related to wealth although *uncorrelated* with the stock market return or asset volatility. That this seems plausible highlights the ability of smart people to model anything into their prejudices because only an insider with a deep understanding of the mathematics of modern finance would think this is both desirable and makes any sense.

As Jonathan Haidt notes about politics, there's a tendency to build a motivated ring of ignorance around sacred assumptions, those assumptions that simultaneously bind and blind a group together. The absolute wealth utility function at the core of economics is just such a sacred assumption, because it is so inconsistent with so much of reality (though importantly, not all). Our tendency to rationalize for some prejudice is natural, though not insurmountable.[182] As Charles Darwin noted,

> False facts are highly injurious to the progress of science, for they often long endure; but false views, if supported by some evidence, do little harm, as everyone takes a salutary pleasure in proving their falseness.[183]

In this case, the false fact is that there is an omnipresent risk premium. The equity risk premium everyone assumes is too big contains many subtractions for your average investor that would, with a different prejudice, be considered highly important. Omitting these adjustments makes sense if you think your assumption, that the risk premium is large and omnipresent, is true.

Many well respected scientists have created seminal empirical results that have been found seriously flawed. Consider Millikan's initial estimation for the mass of an electron, Eddington's measure of the deflection of light via the sun to prove general relativity, Pasteur's attempt to disprove the theory of spontaneous generation of life, Kepler's data on planetary motions—all of which were seminal in promoting important new scientific facts that underlay new important theories. These are giants of science, but posthumously we now know they all tendentiously excluded observations that would have contradicted their ultimate results in ways that would be called fraudulent if they happened to be wrong on the big picture.[184] We are very good at rationalizing our prejudices.[185]

We forgive the Pasteurs and Keplers because they were right, but this highlights that we see what we believe, and it is more important to have the correct biases than an objective and meticulous methodology. All data are noisy, but we make excuses why letting in data that fit our theory is right and why we should exclude data that does not fit our theory. Our prejudices guide how we tendentiously adjust the data until to get the results we expect.

For example, the initial empirical study of beta on stocks was by George Douglas (1969), and he found residual variance was correlated with returns, not beta. Merton Miller and Myron Scholes (1972), two economists who would later win the Nobel Prize for independent theoretical work, pointed out several flaws in Douglas's empirical work. They found Douglas's result was greatly diminished, but not eliminated, by accounting for

- Changing interest rates
- Changes in volatility
- Measurement errors in beta
- Correlations between residual volatility and beta
- An inadequate proxy for the market
- Cross-sectional correlation in residual errors
- Correlation between skewness and volatility

Alas, they did not include size or price, which would have highlighted that the sign goes the opposite way. A year later, seminal work found the positive beta-return relation but only after a process of correcting for "errors in variables," where high betas are invariably positively biased, low betas have a negative bias. This is a sensible adjustment, but the key is that when this trick was applied and the expected answer came out (higher beta, higher returns), top researchers basically left this result unchallenged for twenty years. In general smart people are good at rationalizing their prejudices, and here a great deal of biases were controlled for until the expected answer came out (i.e., beta positively correlated with return), and the glaring biases that went the other way—overestimating returns to low-priced stocks and the delisting bias to highly volatile firms—were not addressed for decades.

Stephen Cecchetti's textbook *Money, Banking, and Financial Markets* immediately presents the seemingly straightforward example of how bonds with higher default rates have higher yields: risk and expected return are positively correlated. Yet this is purely an anticipation of the default rates so is not risk in the sense of something priced. BBB bonds have, over time, the same total return as B-rated bonds, in spite of the fact that yields for B-rated bonds are always higher than for BBB-rated bonds. One must subtract the expected defaults and the resulting losses from a stated yield regardless of one's risk tolerance. Confusing stated yield with return is a simple, obvious error. The distinction between the amortized expected loss from defaults and priced risk is a fundamental distinction in modern risk-return theory. The usage of expected loss risk as opposed to 'risk premium' risk when it generates intuitive support at 30,000 feet suggests that financial professionals have a strong, active bias toward the big idea: risk begets average returns.[186] This is the kind of rationalization people make when they are certain their big picture is correct.

Everyone knows that a little inaccuracy can save a lot of explanation, so this is always tempting, but this gets to the heart of finance, the essence of the risk premium. The little lie implicit in Cecchetti's illustration is symptomatic of how top-level academics are misleading their students based on the good intention that their principle—that risk underlies expected returns—is important and true. Esteemed academics aren't consciously lying but making little misrepresentations so their students can see the important point about risk premiums. Unfortunately, these wishful misrepresentations pervade the entire field.

8.3 Sophisticated Analysis

Economics in general, and finance in particular, is a science with a vast array of specialization. A lot of effort is put into sophisticated methods, such as the generalized method of moments, or deriving pricing functions via first order conditions from some utility function. The most esteemed financial econometrics in the 1980s was work by Shanken, Gibbons, and Ross that used maximum likelihood functions to estimate betas and expected returns simultaneously. These models were very abstract but corrected flaws in the earlier approaches to address measurement error in beta. Yet all it took was a simple cross-tabbing of beta with size, presented by credible insiders, to convince most people the standard CAPM model was untenable. The focus of financial academics has been on econometric methods that have been irrelevant to key discoveries of the past 50 years.

Interestingly, the data I present here is a good example of evidence that is too unwieldy for a refereed journal. Academics like rigorous tests using a small set of econometric tests on single asset classes, so the error structure needs to be very particular to that asset class (e.g., taking into account the heteroskedasticity of equity markets). These tests generally do not generalize to other asset classes, and are especially irrelevant applied to several very different assets classes, so the survey approach presented here simply does not conform to any academic journal. Some facts—like the low return on intraday versus overnight returns or penny stocks—are so simple, extended analysis would only obscure them, yet most asset classes will have critics who claim my data are being tortured in the wrong way because in general the data are complex enough to generate different results if you use different time periods, exclusion rules, and other factors. I think the confluence of many independent facts is most compelling, including such diverse cues as the lack of value of beta in mutual funds, the failure of Miller-Modigliani in both equity and debt returns, and the relative pervasiveness of physics PhDs over finance PhDs working in hedge funds.

In an early comment on the failure of the CAPM, Shanken and Smith argued for standard solution:

> Scientific knowledge rarely proceeds by completely abandoning the current framework, rather, it proceeds by modifying the framework and broadening our understanding to embrace the anomalies, while retaining that which currently fits.[187]

After twenty years, this wishfulness has led nowhere and should be abandoned. A major problem is that as most of the active and esteemed researchers have built their careers extending or modifying the current framework, it would be very costly to classify work built on bad assumptions as irrelevant, and so there is this strong desire to work within the paradigm and salvage all those mentor's reputations. Yet the problem in asset pricing theory is not some second-order refinement, some inconsistency that occurs at extremes; rather, the entire framework is based on a profound mistake over what is more important to financial decision makers, envy versus greed. There is an alluring inner consistency to any worldview developed by scholars over generations, but that does not mean it is true, it merely means that it survives as an ideology because it can explain everything and thus nothing. We should be applying the more pragmatic goal for our theories, the acceptance of what predicts better, and the rejection of what predicts worse.

8.4 Epilogue: My Anecdote

My 1994 dissertation centered on the low returns to highly volatile equities, which then I argued was related to the incentives and preferences individuals had toward buying highly volatile stocks. The thesis and the meta strategy behind the thesis did not generate much interest among finance professors at my school, and word-of-mouth recommendations as important in this field as any other, I received zero job offers from academia. A portion of my dissertation that did not concern asset returns was published in the *Journal of Finance*, so it was not as though it were simply a bad piece of research; it merely was not perceived as potentially interesting by the finance profession at that time. Unfortunately, back then I was making a partial equilibrium argument (i.e., no relative utility) long before the Freakonomics craze of the later 1990s, after which any anomaly with a mere wink towards a behavioral motivation was considered worthy of study independent of any arbitrage it might imply. [188]

I was not discouraged. Naively, I thought it was better that academia did not appreciate the insight because I could then apply my insight as a fund manager and generate big profits. I had traded a bit before graduate school and preferred the practical approach anyway. I pitched the idea to buy low-volatility stocks using data from my dissertation to various parties and was always dismissed. Eventually, I took a job as an economist with a regional bank in Cleveland mainly because it offered the potential to collaborate with the bank's asset management group. It turned out that those in charge of portfolio managers were also unmoved by my low-volatility strategy. I was able to find only one venue for presenting my stock findings, at the Cleveland Fed, and it solicited no interest. Basically, they all thought I was wrong, so my low volatility data and my story about an agency problem among fund managers, was irrelevant.

In 1996 while a risk manager, I got special permission by KeyCorp's lead counsel take $120k in family savings that was put into a stand-alone LLC to demonstrate a track record. It went long low-volatility stocks with above-average momentum. After a couple years, it had good returns and a below-average beta, and of course I had data back to 1926 from my dissertation, but when I approached several funds for some real capital, there was no interest. [189] A common complaint in late 1999 was that it was lagging other strategies at that time that were going up several-fold during the Internet bubble, but the most common comment was that if it was a good idea, others would be doing it.

Every year or so I would send an academic version of my papers highlighting the low return to high-risk stocks to well-known academics, and the usual response was silence, the ultimate rejection. Often I would receive a summary rejection from journals, which means they rejected it without even sending it to a referee because it was so obviously unpublishable, and the journal editor would cheerfully remind me my submission fee was fully refunded. One prominent journal told me it was "not accepting new papers at this time," one noted the result was trivial, another told me it was mathematically wrong. One journal simply noted my argument was "not of interest to the general reader of [this financial journal]." I responded that while my argument could be wrong, the idea that risk does not generate an expected return was central to finance, and thus of interest. The editor replied, "I meant, it is not rigorous enough." I sensed he just didn't like it.[190] One colleague forwarded it to a finance professor, who angrily told him not to ever send him such harebrained papers, and noted that I was arguing the world is flat.

Eventually, I did become an equity long-short portfolio manager at a hedge fund. I personally made $3.5MM over two years applying this idea in a way that I cannot describe fully for legal reasons.[191] A peculiar legal entanglement of little interest to anyone but me ensued, focused on my attempt to start a new low-volatility strategy.[192] In one of my court proceedings, their lawyer was asked as to the damages that were potentially at stake, and she replied, "Unknown at this point. It could be tremendous … hundreds of millions of dollars."[193] A rhetorical flourish perhaps, but it highlights people with intimate knowledge of the idea found this insight very valuable.

The bottom line is that this insight has generated successful out-of-sample results to me personally, but was generally not worth consideration among academia and industry. I have seen first-hand how data and theory are treated differently the model of science proffered by Karl Popper, as it is much more like the adoption of political policies based on a vague mixture of evidence and coalitions. I think the eventual interest in low volatility investing was just that after the 1992 Fama-French results were really digested, everyone saw the basic implication that a higher Sharpe was implied for low volatility stocks, and this made low volatility investing inevitable. The truth will eventually be accepted for a variety of reasons, but it takes a while.

CHAPTER 9

Practical Implications

The purpose of wisdom, said Cicero, is to know the good. There should be some good practical implications of an important scientific insight, something that will make you more prosperous. The idea that there is no general risk premium and that highly volatile investments tend to be overbought generates some very useful, simple insights.

9.1 Low-Volatility Investing

As shown in sections 4.1 to 4.3, low-volatility investing generates higher returns at lower volatility, a "twofer" in Sharpe space. I think most people do not invest this way due to benchmarking, but they should. As mentioned, I have employed this process successfully, but as more proof that this strategy is truly feasible and not some in-sample statistical artifact, consider the performance of the major institutional equity managers Acadian, Analytic Investors, Robeco, and Unigestion that have been applying low volatility strategies.

As with my findings and the research of others, these institutions have been generating higher returns than their benchmarks have at around 40 percent less volatility. The low-volatility fund space is probably about $10-20 billion at the beginning of 2012. Thus it is eminently feasible to generate the lower risk, higher returns found in the historical data. This is because low-volatility investing is not a transaction-heavy tactic and does not require short sales that are often difficult, and low-volatility stocks tend to be larger and more liquid.

TABLE 9.1. *Returns to actual low volatility through December 2011*

Firm	Acadian	Analytic	Robeco	Unigestion
Strategy	Global Managed Volatility Equity	U.S. Low Volatility	Institutional Conservative Equity	Global Minimum Variance
Start-Date	A-06	N-04	S-06	D-07
Fund AnnRet(%)	3.65	6.02	0.9	0.2
Relative Vol	0.65	0.76	0.59	0.67
Benchmark	MSCI World (USD)	Russel 1000	MSCI World (Euro)	MSCI Euro
Benchmark AnnRet(%)	0.0	4.0	-0.6	-7.76

Since around the year 2000, every six months I have created MVP portfolios using either fifty or twenty-five constituents from the various indexes. I have then estimated a set of latent factors and have minimized the portfolio variance to those factors, using the historical daily data over the prior year. The results have been portfolios with significantly lower volatility and higher returns. This magnitude is shown in Section 4.2 but also is highlighted by the fact that three of the four MVPs second order stochastically dominated the index they were drawn from.[194] That is, using monthly data, all but the MSCI-Europe MVP dominated its index in this way, but using daily data, all but the Nikkei. I computed these tests nonparametrically using actual data, so they are snapshots, but they highlight the massive dominance of these approaches for your stereotypical "mean-variance" investor. Every risk-averse agent should prefer a portfolio that second order stochastically dominates another.

Now, if I were a starting a low-volatility fund I would create a worldwide minimum-variance fund, as opposed to a low-beta fund. The reason is twofold. First, low beta is dominated by a minimum-variance portfolio. Here are statistics from 1998 on low, beta 0.5, and MVP portfolios for the United States

TABLE 9.2. *US MVP versus low-beta portfolios United States: January 1998–December 2011*

	Beta-Low	MVP
GeoMean	6.2%	9.0%
AnnStDev	15.9%	12.4%
Beta	0.61	0.47
Sharpe	0.21	0.49

Interestingly, the MVP portfolio had a lower beta than the approach that simply grabbed the lowest beta stocks. This could be because the MVP I created was constrained to be within the S&P 500, which is sort of an outside-the-box beta modifier. Also the volatility unrelated to the CAPM beta is probably correlated, prospectively, with future beta loadings, and so this approach incidentally targets lower beta better than simply taking those stocks with the lowest betas.

The second reason to form such a portfolio is that diversification makes the appeal of the *worldwide* MVP even better. That is, if you buy into the logic that MVPs are good because they have a dominant Sharpe ratio and are less correlated with your stock market, this point is only exaggerated for the diversified portfolio of MVPs. That is, returns should not go down moving from Japan to the United States or vice versa, in that with arbitrage, I expect the return on all passive indexes to be about the same. So the return (numerator of Sharpe) is the same, but with the power of diversification, the volatility is reduced. Here are the results for the total returns on a worldwide MVP focus versus simply equal weighting the four major equity indexes.

As you can see, the MVPs portfolio outperformed the simple index approach, generating a nice 3.3 percent annualized return premium, all with 35 percent less volatility. So in the same way that one can improve an index via an MVP, one can improve an MVP via a portfolio of worldwide MVPs.

FIGURE 9.1. *Total return to MVPs versus worldwide indexes: January 2001–December 2012*

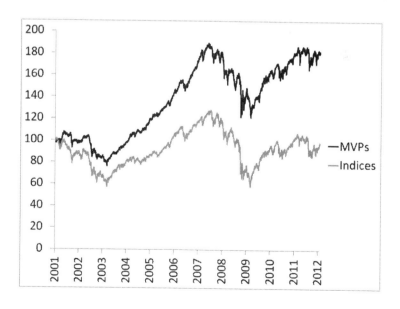

Again, we see lower volatility, higher return. For the Sharpe maximizing investor, not having liquid international exposure makes zero sense because these exposures are the ultimate free lunch. The performance of MVPs, including how these were created, is explained in Section 4.2, and one can see there for details. To recap, the annualized volatility can be reduced by one-third within these indexes by simply reweighting the constituents in a way that minimizes the historical volatility using a factor minimization algorithm on prior returns, which is then applied to generate the out-of-sample returns. Furthermore, in each case, the numerator of the Sharpe ratio was also significantly higher; returns averaged 3.5 percent annualized above the index from which the MVP portfolio was created.

9.2 A Mid Beta Portfolio

If one is concerned about benchmark risk and avoiding lagging the market, one could form a portfolio with only stocks that have betas near 1.0, generating a portfolio with a beta near 1 but without the high flyers and really low-beta stocks. This generates a 2 percent to 3 percent lift annually because (1) there is a slight increase in returns from low to medium betas/volatility and (2) the high betas/volatility are where the real loser stocks are, and these are avoided. As most investors benchmark and are wary of deviating too much from the average market beta, this approach plays more into their preference to have an average market exposure. Indeed, this would be a great closet indexing strategy, in that many funds are accused of secretively aping the indexes and reaping large fees for merely giving investors a story that they have some grand strategy behind their equity portfolio, something more bold and thoughtful than passive index investing. A smart manager should realize his odds at successful selective stock picking are poor, and so by applying the mid beta approach—grabbing only those stocks with betas near, say within 0.15 of 1.0—they can beat the index rather easily.

A mid beta approach is superior to indexes and active managers for the simple reasons that (1) its eminently feasible and (2) it avoids the inferior highly risky equities.

FIGURE 9.2. *Annual returns to S&P 500, MVP, and Mid Beta*

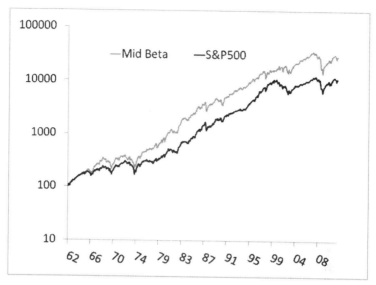

One can download all these data from my website, www.betaarbitrage.com.

9.3 Sundry

A simple take-away is that higher risk assets are generally bad investments: high risk stocks, bonds, currencies, generate at best the same expected return for twice the volatility. This generalizes to all sorts of assets and strategies:[195]

- in distressed debt, seniors easily beat subordinated;
- in reinsurance, a rebalanced portfolio beats a peak-peril portfolio;
- in convertibles, high-moneyness bonds beat more speculative low-moneyness bonds;
- in merger arbitrage, more defensive stock-financed acquisitions give better risk-adjusted returns than cash-financed ones; and
- highly volatile times generate lower risk-adjusted returns than less volatile times.

As a general rule it is fruitful to assume risky assets and times are inferior and only invest in them given some truly unique, valuable, insight.

Some of the best investments are the ones we never make. If the method is fruitless and complicated, as the risk premium model is, this wastes time one could spend on something productive. Avoiding modern asset pricing theory will give you more time to learn programming, statistics, or some other useful skill that then gets you into a field you find interesting and then learn the parochial issues that dominate any business. Most valuable creativity is highly domain specific, so while you need a base of basic analytical tools to analyze a problem, ultimately you need a lot of persistent, specialized focus.

Another financial implication is that because returns are not functions of some objective risk measure, risk management as a science will always fail at becoming primal for asset allocation. When I was head of economic capital allocations at KeyCorp, the field was just developing. The hope was that this new science was going to take risk management from an audit-type function to one more offensive, more important. This never happened. There is no objective risk metric that allows one to compare a real estate to a credit card portfolio. Most of the valuable advantages in a business are parochial issues where business line managers with their stronger focus will strictly dominate any strategic insights from some general trend seen by the professional risk managers. The only risk, equal across all asset classes, that one can see from way up high are simple things like too much counterparty exposure. These are rarely risks essential for a prescient strategy; rather, they are signs of simple malfeasance (operational risk such as rogue traders exceeding their limits). Thus risk management as a separate business line will always be like audit, and the better this is understood, the better it will work.

One of the biggest successes of economics is derivatives pricing, and, interestingly, the key insight there is that via arbitrage the risk-adjusted return is irrelevant. One, therefore, can use risk neutral pricing and just discount the expected payoffs via the LIBOR curve or whatever your funding rate is. Prices are determined independent of their covariance with the spooky risk factor, which is a nice thing given no one knows what that is. This field has been very successful precisely because it does not get sidetracked by risk premiums. I'm just suggesting that one should do this in all of one's investments, not just derivatives. In practice, this is what is done, as any strategy that generates persistent above-average returns (small cap stocks, value stocks, selling futures in contango) is generally presumed to be attractive. Throughout my career, if something made money after some unadjusted cost of funding and amortized expected loss, we did it.[196]

One key risk management implication is that any strategy or asset with a high yield is like a junk bond. The small probability of a large loss can make all these high yielding strategies have equal expected yields, which highlights the importance of estimating an extreme event in those cases. In contrast, with risk premiums one could assume the yields are indicative of higher expected returns, all due to risk, highlighting the complacency the standard approach encourages.

An important point about finance is the great amount of deception that goes on. The value of any investor resides in intangible property that is costless to reproduce. Consider the strategies of pairs trading or convertible bond arbitrage. Both strategies could be explained to a smart person in five minutes. Now, if you knew this in 1992 when both strategies had ten years of easy money ahead of them and tried to get hired to do it by describing it in full, surely many potential employers would thank you for your visit, decline, then do this themselves. I personally know of several cases where this happened, so it is not a hypothetical.[197] Consider why so many people were comfortable investing with infamous Ponzi scammer Bernie Madoff even though his stated strategy was patently infeasible at the size of his assets under management. Most investors did not care because they presumed he was doing something other than what he said, as all fund managers do.[198] Investors have gotten used to telling and hearing white lies.

In such a context, modern risk theory thrives because when someone says the special sauce is risk management, they need not be clear because current theory is not clear. I have literally wasted years trying to understand the essence of various businesses lines because their managers promoted some chimerical risk management function that was simply a pretext for their doing something much more prosaic.

Gary Gorton makes this observation about the hedge fund industry:

"The founder has a secret. Either the secret is that the founder has no new ideas. Or, the founder's secret is a new idea. If the founder has no new idea, that cannot be revealed. If the founder has an original idea, he also can't share it with investors because they might steal it."[199]

I can attest to this problem and would say almost every investor misleadingly represents his alpha in published interviews or even private conversation with clients, in ways that are both more flattering (e.g., elegant and profound) and do not give away valuable information. Now, these aren't lies so much as very selective stories; like all good salesmen, they really believe what they say.[200]

I described some of the games played in this dimension in my book *Finding Alpha*, and the fundamental issue is that truth telling is rarely an optimal strategy.[201] The key is they are taking money out of the system in places that do not show up in simple reports, always sure to present the most favorable yet still plausible benchmark. Effective fraudsters are like magicians, directing attention away from where the money is being taken. In my experience, most financial professionals pitching a service or strategy harbor material misrepresentations, which is why stupid investors lose money so surely. Unfortunately, all investors get taken some of the time; for example, I bought a whole life insurance policy that probably generated more fee income than anything I will ever buy. The risk premium encourages misleading presentations by claiming some ethereal risk premium makes almost any price plausible; however, if one assumed a zero risk premium you can assess claims much more objectively (eg, one would presume a large, small-probability losses for *anything* with a large current yield).

One major implication of this insight is that if we should expect returns to be more than what is suggested via standard LIBOR rates, many public sector pensions are severely underfunded. A total of 60 percent of defined benefit pensions are in equities, and they generally assume pensions have assumed risk premiums built into their returns of around 5 percent. I argue this is implausibly high, and given the lower transaction costs to retail investors, the historical top-line returns are probably biased upwards, because it is the net return to all investors that the equity markets are equilibrating. If I'm right, many governmental pension plans simply will not have the assets needed for their obligations, and have to either raise revenues or cut services. I imagine they will default on bond payments before cutting pension benefits, but this makes the problem worse because many of their assets are in bonds, which would then fall in value. Think of it as a positive feedback loop in the no-equity risk premium hypothesis.

If we are primarily driven by relative status, this implies our society will never reach the bliss point anticipated by Keynes in his essay "Possibilities for our Grandchildren," where he imagined several more generations of income growth would leave people mainly concerned with how to spend their leisure time.[202] That has not happened and never will, as people will always be anxious about climbing the status ladder. Constantly climbing a status ladder may sound base, but a dominant strategy is the Dale Carnegie method of winning friends and influencing people: be empathetic, nice, and helpful to others.[203] The goal of finding one's best role to generate one's greatest status fits in nicely with the Japanese concept of ikigai and the Serenity Prayer, both salutary principles.[204]

Clearly envy can be taken too far, as when the Navajo Indians reportedly had no concept of luck or of personal achievement and so believed that one person's success can only come at another's expense. This created intense envy towards those better off, and discouraged people from adopting better ways of growing crops or making other improvements.[205] Then there were the many genocides committed, not against the poor but rather the prosperous: Armenians in Turkey, Chinese in Indonesia, Kulaks in Russia, of course Jews in Germany. That envy has a dark side hardly needs elaborating, but this is like any of our instincts, good only in moderation.

While good investments do involve risk, they also involve a deep knowledge of the particular circumstances of time and place and then some kind of analogy or generalization that others have not made. Finding good investments is like finding good ideas in general, things that are new, true, and important, and to reduce this to one dimension—a covariance with a something objective—is absurd. As an investor, you should try to remove intuitively risky assets from your passive indexes. If you still are looking for something that will make you rich passively, at least be aware risk taking on average costs, it does not pay.

CHAPTER 10

Conclusion

A good life is filled with precious moments, prized accomplishments, and loving relationships, all of which involve some kind of risk taking. Risk is clearly a necessary condition for many things that give us profound satisfaction, but this does not imply risk is a sufficient condition for good returns in any sense. On average, gambling is an expense, and the riskier gambles cost more than the safer ones. This is a better description of asset markets in general than the current paradigm, which states that risk and expected returns are in a karmic trade-off and that passive investing has an expected return above simple LIBOR rates. Many common investment strategies and tactics are as costly as gambling, often presented disingenuously, abetted by standard theory that confines such practices to anomalies.

Omnipresent risk premiums are implied by globally concave utility functions, and seemingly proved by the equity risk premium which seems very large. Yet the empirical support for a priced risk premium is absent across a large spectrum of investable assets. The empirical anomalies to the positive risk- return theory are not exceptions to a general tendency. There is no general tendency within a variety of investments such as equities, options, most of the yield curve, high-yield corporate and bankrupt bonds, mutual funds, commodities, small business owners, movies, lottery tickets, and horse races. Indeed, many high-risk assets actually have lower-than-average returns, as with high-beta/volatility stocks, IPOs, currencies, or lotteries.

When Harry Markowitz presented his dissertation, which outlined how to construct the efficient frontier that supposedly defined portfolios everyone should be interested in, one of his advisers was Milton Friedman, who half-seriously commented that the dissertation was not on economics but rather operations research. Markowitz mentioned this disrespectful anecdote in his Nobel lecture forty years later, surely the ultimate revenge, because nothing stings like the lukewarm approval of men we respect.

As the vast majority of Markowitz's early work focused on algorithms to identify efficient frontier portfolios given various expected returns, and now portfolio volatility is considered at best unrelated with expected returns, these algorithms are all rather quaint. In that sense, Friedman's intuition has been vindicated, as with hindsight the efficient frontier in return-standard deviation space has nothing to do with risk according to the latest general equilibrium models. Markowitz's lasting idea was merely the benefits of diversification, which is a good idea but simple enough and hardly novel.

There's always the hope that a long-standing problem, like Fermat's last theorem, is merely waiting for the right complex proof, which would include ideas that require a great amount of specialized technical knowledge. This would not only validate the problem, but also the tools needed to solve the problem, presumably those that top academics use in their latest research. Great classical music is an example of something that validates rigorous study because if you study such music rigorously, you do appreciate it more. Alas, it rarely works that way, as most good ideas about how to behave are rather simple: be nice, don't be a pushover, only take risks in areas where you have a comparative advantage. The difficulty in applying these simple rules is because any specific application involves balance to a specific situation (e.g., be nice but not a pushover).

Remember the findings of Diether et al (2002), who found analyst estimate dispersion is positively related to beta, volatility, and earnings variability. Yet because the average return correlation went the wrong way, they noted, "Our results clearly reject the notion that dispersion in forecasts can be viewed as a proxy of risk." So in spite of being correlated with all things intuitively risky, like beta, volatility, and size, but uncorrelated with value or momentum, the correlation with returns suggests to these researchers that analyst uncertainty cannot be correlated with risk because the one thing they know about risk is that it is positively correlated with returns. This is where the risk premium assumptions lead one, to snipe hunts for risk factors.[206] Such thinking is common and demonstrates researchers are very eager and proficient at rationalizing their paradigm, but it will highlight a strange madness of our times.[207]

The belief that risk properly measured must be positively related to returns is very deep among academics. Risk is supposedly not only important and everywhere but also subtle, requiring that investors implicitly have skills similar in sophistication and imprecision to what is needed to distinguish between a good and great wine. As an alternative, the irrelevance of risk to return is implied by a status-conscious investor benchmarking himself against others and holds in both a utility and arbitrage argument. Risk is simply allocating an unusual amount of wealth to any asset that would generate a significant deviation from the market portfolio.

The implications of this approach are profound. We should expect never to see a robust metric of something positively correlated with our wealth's volatility that is positively related to average returns. One should treat expected returns the way derivative pricing does, as some trivial correspondence to a LIBOR curve.

The sad fact of investing is that it pays to be smart and it costs to be stupid. At every point in the process, various costs pull from the top-line returns to any investment so that after a while the insiders are getting all the abnormal returns to any asset class and generate mere risk-free returns to investors. One must monitor these investment managers or do it themselves to fully take advantage of any above-average risk-reward opportunity. Unfortunately, this will always involve a lot of domain specific knowledge, so it does not lend itself to a curriculum.[208] The smartness that helps investing is weakly correlated with the formal educational tools one learns in modern finance, and is more related to intuitions that are called common sense. The current risk paradigm prioritizes analytical tools that have no empirical support while downplaying the intuition that really dominates the search for alpha.

The standard model generates a good normative objective to maximize Sharpe ratios as much as possible, but this takes us only so far because most people care more about deviations from the benchmark. A relative wealth orientation generates a more accurate positive theory, and its assumption is generally considered more accurate by those doing research on the essence of subjective well-being. The relative status utility function generates a more accurate description of the world.

Beta is still descriptive of relative volatility and generates normative guidance for volatility minimization, which I believe *should* be a priority. However, there is no robust cross-sectional return to any β, no upward sloping security market line. The portfolio optimization algorithm for an investor with typical preferences is trivial and mimics practice: allocate assets to the standard categories of conventional wisdom because this minimizes relative wealth volatility. You can, and I believe should, raise your Sharpe by avoiding those subsets of asset classes that are most risky, and even times that are most risky, but that itself takes a little risk because risk is doing something different.

A contingent path-dependency has created a nonfalsifiable framework for analyzing investments that is mainly irrelevant, but deeply entrenched. Change is coming, however, as acceptance of low volatility investing has moved related arguments from indefensible to legitimate, purely as a function of the zeitgeist. Yet this particular anomaly is just the tip of the iceberg, and underneath it are the many empirical ramifications of a flawed utility assumption. The greatest benefit to this insight is to waste less time, avoid assets with objectively bad returns, and focus on the parochial issues that can make you more prosperous.

Bibliography

Abel, Andrew B. 1990. "Asset Prices Under Habit Formation and Catching up with the Joneses." *American Economic Review* 80 (2): 38–42.

Allais, M. 1953."Le Comportement de l'Homme Rationnel Devant le Risque: Critique des Postulats et Axiomes de l'école Américaine." *Econometrica* 21 (4): 503–546.

Altman, Edward, and William Stonberg. 2006. "The Market in Defaulted Bonds and Bank Loans." *Journal of Portfolio Management* 32(4): 93–105.

Altman, Edward, and Gaurav Bana. 2004. "Defaults and Returns on High-Yield Bonds." *Journal of Portfolio Management* 30 (2): 58–72.

Amromin, Gene, and Steven A. Sharpe. 2005). "From the Horse's Mouth: Gauging Conditional Expected Stock Returns from Investor Survey." AFA 2006 Boston Meetings Paper, SSRN: http://ssrn.com/abstract=686944.

Ariely, D. 2008. *Predictably Irrational: The Hidden Forces that Shape Our Decisions.* New York: HarperCollins.

Avramov, Doron, and Russ Wermers. 2000. "Investing in Mutual Funds When Returns Are Predictable." *Journal of Financial Economics* 81 (2): 339–377.

Bansal, R., and C. Lundblad. 2002. "Market efficiency, fundamental values, and asset returns in global equity markets," *Journal of Econometrics* 109: 195–237.

Bansal, Ravi, and Yaron, Amir. 2004. "Risks for the Long Run: A Potential Resolution of Asset Pricing Puzzles." *Journal of Finance* 59 (4): 1481–1509.

Barber, Brad, and Terrance Odean. 1999. "The Courage of Misguided Convictions: The Trading Behavior of Individual Investors." *Financial Analyst Journal* 55 (6): 41–55.

————. 2000. "Trading Is Hazardous to Your Wealth: The Common Stock Investment Performance of Individual Investors." *The Journal of Finance* 55 (2): 773–806.

Basu, S. 1977. "Investment Performance of Common Stocks in Relation to Their Price-Earnings Ratios: A Test of the Efficient Market Hypothesis." *Journal of Finance* 32 (3): 663–682.

Bentley, Alex, Mark Earls, Michael O'Brien, and John Maeda. 2011. *I'll Have What She's Having: Mapping Social Behavior.* Cambridge: The MIT Press.

Bhandari, L. C. 1988. "Debt/Equity Ratio and Expected Common Stock Returns: Empirical Evidence." *Journal of Finance* 43 (2): 507–528.

Bhardwaj, Geetesh, Gary B. Gorton, and K. Geert Rouwenhorst. 2008. "Fooling Some of the People All of the Time: The Inefficient Performance and Persistence of Commodity Trading Advisors." NBER Working Papers 14424, National Bureau of Economic Research, Inc.

Bhattacharyya, N., and Thomas Garrett. 2006. *"Why People Choose Negative Expected Return Assets-an Empirical Examination of a Utility Theoretic Explanation."* Federal Reserve Bank of St. Louis.

Black, F. 1993. "Estimating Expected Return." *Financial Analysts Journal* 49: 36–36.

Blitz, David, and Pim van Vliet. 2007. "The Volatility Effect: Lower Risk Without Lower Return." *Journal of Portfolio Management* 102–113.

Blume, M., and I. A. Friend. 1973. "A New Look at the Capital Asset Pricing Model." *Journal of Finance* 28: 19–33.

Blume, M. E., and R F. Stambaugh. 1983. "An Application to the Size Effect." *Journal of Financial Economics* 12: 387–404.

Bostrom, Nick. 2003. "Are You Living in a Computer Simulation?" *Philosophical Quarterly* 53(211): 243–255.

Burnside, A. Craig, Martin S. Eichenbaum, Isaac Kleshchelski, and Sergio Rebelo. 2009. "Do Peso Problems Explain the Returns to the Carry Trade?" NBER Working Paper No. 14054, National Bureau of Economic Research, Inc.

Cai, Tao Tony, and Qiu, Mei. 2009. "International Evidence on Overnight Return." SSRN: http://ssrn.com/abstract=1524013.

Campbell, John Y., Robert J. Shiller, and Luis M. Viceira. 2009. "Understanding Inflation-Indexed Bond Markets." Cowles Foundation Discussion Paper No. 1696. SSRN: http://ssrn.com/abstract=1406500.

Campbell, John Y., Jens Hilscher, and Jan Szilagyi. 2008. "In Search of Distress Risk." *Journal of Finance* 63: 2899–2939.

Carhart, M. 1997. "On Persistence in Mutual Fund Performance." *Journal of Finance* 52: 57–82.

Chen, N. F., R. Roll, and S. A. Ross. 1986. "Economic Forces and the Stock Market." *Journal of Business* 59 (3): 383.

Clarke, Roger, Harindra de Silva, and Steven Thorley. 2006. "Minimum-Variance Portfolio in the U.S. Equity Market." *Journal of Portfolio Management* 37 (2): 10–24.

Coval, J. D, and T. Shumway. 2001. "Expected Option Returns." *The Journal of Finance* 56 (3): 983–1009.

Cox, J., J. Ingersoll, and S. Ross. 1985. "An Intertemporal General Equilibrium Model of Asset Prices." *Econometrica* 53: 363–384.

Daniel, Kent, and Sheridan Titman. 1998. "Characteristics or Covariances?" *Journal of Portfolio Management* 24 (4): 24–33.

Davis, Morris A., and Jonathan Heathcote. 2007. "The Price and Quantity of Residential Land in the United States." *Journal of Monetary Economics* 54 (8): 2595–2620.

De Bondt, Werner F. M., and Richard H. Thaler. 1985. "Does the Stock Market Overreact?" *Journal of Finance* 40: 793–806.

———. 1987. "Further Evidence on Investor Overreaction and Stock Market Seasonality." *Journal of Finance* 42: 557–581.

De Long, J. Bradford, Andrei Shleifer, Lawrence H. Summers, and Robert J. Waldmann. 1990. "Noise Trader Risk in Financial Markets." *Journal of Political Economy* 98(4): 703–38.

De Vany, Arthur S. 2004. *Hollywood Economics: How Extreme Uncertainty Shapes the Film Industry*. Routledge.

De Vany, Arthur S., and David W. Walls. 2002. "Does Hollywood Make Too Many R-Rated Movies?: Risk, Stochastic Dominance, and the Illusion Of Expectation." *The Journal of Business* 75 (3): 425–451.

DeMarzo, Peter, Ron Kaniel, and Ilan Kremer. 2004. "Diversification as a Public Good: Community Effects in Portfolio Choice." *Journal of Finance* 59: 1677–1715.

Dichev, Ilia D., and Gwen Yu. 2011. "Higher Risk, Lower Returns: What Hedge Fund Investors Really Earn." *Journal of Financial Economics* 100 (2): 248–263.

Dichev, Ilia. 1998. "Is the Risk of Bankruptcy a Systematic Risk?" *Journal of Finance* 53: 1131–1148.

———. 2007. "What Are Stock Investors Actual Historical Returns? Evidence from Dollar Weighted Returns." *American Economic Review* 97: 386–401.

Diether, K. B., C. J. Malloy, and A. Scherbina. 2002. "Differences of Opinion and the Cross Section of Stock Returns." *The Journal of Finance* 57 (5): 2113–2141.

Dimson, Elroy, Paul Marsh, and Mike Staunton. 2006. "The Worldwide Equity Premium: A Smaller Puzzle." EFA 2006 Zurich Meetings Paper; AFA 2008 New Orleans Meetings Paper. SSRN: http://ssrn.com/abstract=891620.

Douglas, G. W. 1969. "Risk In The Equity Markets: An Empirical Appraisal of Market Efficiency." *Yale Economic Essays* 9: 3–45.

Easterlin, Richard A. 1974. "Does Economic Growth Improve the Human Lot? Some Empirical Evidence." In Paul A. David and Melvin W. Reder, eds., *Nations and Households in Economic Growth: Essays in Honor of Moses Abramovitz*, New York: Academic Press, Inc.

Ellsberg, Daniel. 1961. "Risk, Ambiguity, and the Savage Axioms." *Quarterly Journal of Economics* 75 (4): 643–669.

Eraker, Bjorn, and Ready, Mark J. 2011. "Do Investors Overpay for Stocks with Lottery-Like Payoffs? An Examination of the Returns on OTC Stocks." SSRN: http://ssrn.com/abstract=1733225.

Erb, C. B., and C. R. Harvey. 2006. "The Strategic and Tactical Value of Commodity Futures." *Financial Analysts Journal* 62 (2): 69–97.

Faber, Mebane T., and Eric W. Richardson. 2009. *The Ivy Portfolio.* Wiley.

Falkenstein, Eric. 2009. *Finding Alpha: The Search for Alpha when Risk and Return Break Down.* Wiley Finance.

———. 2009b. "Risk and Return in General: Theory and Evidence." Available at SSRN: http://ssrn.com/abstract=1420356.

———. 1996. "Preferences for Stock Characteristics as Revealed by Mutual Fund Portfolio Holdings." *Journal of Finance* 51 (1): 111–135.

———. 1994. "Mutual Funds, Idiosyncratic Variance, and Asset Returns." PhD diss. Northwestern University. Available at http://www.efalken.com/papers/efdiss94.pdf.

Fama, Eugene. 1991. "Efficient Capital Markets." *Journal of Finance* 46: 1575–1617.

Fama, Eugene, and J. MacBeth. 1973. "Risk, Return, and Equilibrium: Empirical Tests." *Journal of Political Economy* 81 (3): 607.

Fama, Eugene, and Kenneth French. 1992. "The Cross-Section of Expected Stock Returns." *Journal of Finance* 47 (2): 427–465.

Fisher, Kenneth L., Jennifer Chou, and Lara W. Hofrmans. 2007. *The Only Three Questions that Count: Investing by Knowing What Others Don't.* Hoboken, NJ: John Wiley.

Frank, Robert. 2011. *The Darwin Economy: Liberty, Competition, and the Common Good.* Princeton University Press.

Friedman, M., and L. J. Savage. 1948. "The Utility Analysis of Choices Involving Risk." *The Journal of Political Economy* 56 (4): 279.

Gali, Jordi. 1995. "Keeping up with the Joneses: Consumption Externalities, Portfolio Choices, and Asset Prices." *Journal of Money, Credit, and Banking* 26: 1–8.

Garrett, T. A., and R. S. Sobel. 2004. "State Lottery Revenue: The Importance of Game Characteristics." *Public Finance Review* 32 (3): 313–330.

Gazzaniga, Michael S. 2011. *Who's in Charge?: Free Will and the Science of the Brain.* New York, NY: Ecco.

Gibbons, M. R. 1982. "Multivariate Tests of Financial Models: A New Approach." *Journal of Financial Economics* 10 (1): 3–27.

Gibbons, M. R., Steven A Ross, and J. Shanken. 1989. "A Test of the Efficiency of a Given Portfolio." *Econometrica* 57 (5): 1121–1152.

Glosten, L, R., Jagannathan, and D. Runkle. 1993. "On the relation between the expected value and the volatility of the nominal excess return on stocks," *Journal of Finance* 48:1779-1801.

Griffith, R. M. 1949. "Odds Adjustments by American Horse-Race Bettors." *American Journal of Psychology* 62 (August): 290–294.

Hanson, Norwood Russel. 1958. *Patterns of Discovery: An Inquiry into the Conceptual Foundations of Science.* Cambridge University Press.

Haugen, Robert A., and Nardin L. Baker. 1991. "The Efficient Market Inefficiency of Capitalization-Weighted Stock Portfolios." *Journal of Portfolio Management* 17 (3): 35–40.

Hayek, F. A. 1945. "The Use of Knowledge in Society." *American Economic Review* 35 (4): 519–553

Ibbotson, Roger G., Peng Chen, and Kevin X. Zhu. 2010. "The ABCs of Hedge Funds: Alphas, Betas, and Costs." SSRN: http://ssrn.com/abstract=1581559.

Ilmanen, Antti. 2011. *Expected Returns: An Investor's Guide to Harvesting Market Rewards.* Wiley.

Insel, T. R., and R. D. Fernald (2004): "How the Brain Processes Social Information: Searching for the Social Brain," *Annual Review of Neuroscience* 27 (1): 697–722.

Jacobs, K., and K. Wang. 2004. "Idiosyncratic Consumption Risk and the Cross Section of Asset Returns." *The Journal of Finance* 59 (5): 2211–2252.

Jagannathan R., and Z. Wang. 1993. *"The CAPM Is Alive and Well.* Federal Reserve Bank of Minneapolis.

Jagannathan, R., and Y. Wang. 2007. Lazy Investors, Discretionary Consumption, and the Cross-Section of Stock Returns." *The Journal of Finance* 62 (4): 1623–1661.

Jagannathan, R., and Z. Y. Wang. 1996. "The Conditional CAPM and the Cross-Section of Expected Returns." *Journal of Finance* 51 (1): 3–53.

Jegadeesh, N., and S. Titman. 1993. "Returns to Buying Winners and Selling Losers: Implications for Stock Market Efficiency." *Journal of Finance* 48: 65–65.

Keynes, John Maynard. 1930. "The Economic Possibilities of our Grandchildren." In *The Collected Writings of JM Keynes, Vol IX*. London: Macmillan for The Royal Economic Society.

————. 1930. *A Treatise on Money*, London, New York.

Kozhemiakin, A. 1997. "The Risk Premium of Corporate Bonds." *Journal of Portfolio Management* 101–109.

Lakonishok, S., R. W., Andrei Shleifer, and Robert Vishny. 1994. "Contrarian Investment, Extrapolation, and Risk." *Journal of Finance* 49 (5): 1541–1578.

Lettau, M, and S. Ludvigson. 2001. "Consumption, Aggregate Wealth, and Expected Stock Returns." *The Journal of Finance* 56 (3): 815–849.

Levy, Haim, Thierry Post, and Pim van Vliet. 2008. "Downside Risk and Asset Pricing." *Journal of Banking and Finance* 32 (7): 1178–1187.

Lucas, R. 1978. "Asset Prices in an Exchange Economy." *Econometrica* 46 (6): 1429–1445.

Malkiel, B. G., and A. Saha. 2005. "Hedge Funds: Risk and Return." *Financial Analysts Journal* 61 (6): 80.

Markowitz, Harry. 1952. "Portfolio Selection." *Journal of Finance* 7 (1): 77–91.

Maymin, Philip, and Gregg S. Fisher. 2011. "Past Performance is Indicative of Future Beliefs, Risk and Decision Analysis." Forthcoming. NYU Poly Research Paper.

Mehra, R., and E. C. Prescott. 1985. "The Equity Premium: A Puzzle." *Journal of Monetary Economics* 15 (2): 145–161.

Merton, R. C. 1971. "Optimum Consumption and Portfolio Rules in a Continuous-Time Model." *Journal of Economic Theory* 3 (4): 373–413.

Merton, Robert C. 1980. "On Estimating the Expected Return on the Market: An Exploratory Investigation." *Journal of Financial Economics* 8: 1–39.

Miller, Merton H., and Myron Scholes. 1972. "Rates of Return in Relation to Risk: A Re-Examination of Some Recent Findings." *Studies in the Theory of Capital Markets* 47–78.

Modigliani, Franco, and Richard Sutch. 1966. "Innovations in Interest Rate Policy." *American Economic Review* 55 (1/2): 178–197.

Myers, D. G. 2000. *The American Paradox: Spiritual Hunger in an Age of Plenty.* Yale University Press.

Opler, T.C., and S. Titman. 1994. "Financial distress and corporate performance," *Journal of Finance* 49:1015-1015.

Ni, Sophie X. 2007. "Stock Option Returns: A Puzzle." Available at SSRN: http://ssrn.com/abstract=959024.

Pesendorfer, W. 1995. "Design Innovation and Fashion Cycles." *American Economic Review* 85: 771–792.

Phalippou, Ludovic. 2009. "Beware of Venturing into Private Equity." *Journal of Economic Perspectives* 23(1): 147–66.

Phalippou, Ludovic, and Olivier Gottschalg. 2009. "The Performance of Private Equity Funds." *Review of Financial Studies* 22: 1747–1776.

Pink, Dan. 2011. *Drive: The Surprising Truth About What Motivates Us.* New York: Riverhead Trade.

Ramachandran, Vilayanur S.. 2010. *The Tell-Tale Brain: A Neuroscientist's Quest for What Makes Us Human.* W. W. Norton & Co.

Ross, S. A. 1976. "The Arbitrage Pricing Theory of Capital Asset Pricing." *Journal of Economic Theory* 13 (3): 341–360.

Roussanov, Nikolai. 2010. Diversification and Its Discontents: Idiosyncratic and Entrepreneurial Risk in the Quest for Social Status." *Journal of Finance* 65(5): 1755–1788.

Rubinstein, M. 1973. "The Fundamental Theorem of Parameter-Preference Security Valuation." *Journal of Financial and Quantitative Analysis* 8 (1): 61–69.

———. 1974. "An Aggregation Theorem for Securities Markets." *Journal of Financial Economics* 1 (3): 225–244.

Schwartz, Barry. 2004. *The Paradox of Choice: Why More Is Less.* New York: Ecco.

Schwartz, Tal. 2000. "How to Beat the S&P 500 with Portfolio Optimization." Unpublished Manuscript.

Shanken, J. 1985. "Multivariate Tests of the Zero-Beta CAPM." *Journal of Financial Economics* 14 (3): 327–348.

Sharpe, William F. 1964. "Capital Asset Prices: A Theory of Market Equilibrium Under Conditions of Risk." *Journal of Finance* 19 (3): 425–442.

———. 1992. Asset Allocation: Management Style and Performance Measurement." *Journal of Portfolio Management* 18 (2): 7–19.

Snowberg, Erik, and Justin Wolfers. 2010. "Explaining the Favorite-Long Shot Bias: Is It Risk-Love or Misperceptions?" *Journal of Political Economy* 118 (4): 723–745.

Stattman, D. 1980. "Book Values and Stock Returns." *The Chicago MBA: A Journal of Selected Papers* 4: 25–45.

Svenson, O. "Are We All Less Risky and More Skillful Than Our Fellow Drivers?" *Acta Psychologica* 47 (2): 143–148.

Tobin, J. 1958. "Liquidity Preference as Behavior Towards Risk." *Review of Economic Studies* 25 (2): 65–86.

Weitzman, Martin L. 2007. "Subjective Expectations and Asset-Return Puzzles." *American Economic Review* 45 (3): 703–724.

Endnotes

1   See http://www.efalken.com/images/87crash.GIF.

2   The VXX is the long thirty-day VIX futures, which when the front month is much lower than the second month, implies that the position continuously rolls down the futures curve. Thus from January 2009 through November 2010, the VIX lost 45 percent annually, but the VXX lost 70 percent due to contango (contango is when the front month price is below later futures prices).

3   De Long et al., 703–738.

4   For non-English readers, a *red herring* is a distraction, coming from the tactic of using a red herring to take dogs on a wrong track in a foxhunt.

5   This being that an economy or individual is best modeled by a utility function that is increasing in wealth at a decreasing rate, independent of the wealth or income of others. As an example of its importance for many papers, the Diamond and Dybvig (1983) model of bank runs necessitates a risk premium to generate an interesting equilibrium in their model; without it, there is no result, and the paper could not exist.

6   Markowitz (1952), Tobin (1958), Sharpe (1964).

7   L. Fisher and J.H., Lorie (1964): "Rates of return on investments in common stocks," *Journal of Business* 37: 1–21.

8   *Institutional Investor Magazine*, September 1971.

9   The excess return is the return above the risk-free rate.

10   Peter Bernstein. *Against The Gods: The Remarkable Story Of Risk* (New York: Wiley, 1998).

11 M. Rubinstein. *A History of the Theory of Investments: My Annotated Bibliography* (New York, Wiley 2006).

12 Ross (1976): 341-360. Fama and French (2006): 2163-2185

13 In one adjustment explaining the lack of measurement, the earth carries aether with it as it hurls through space, confounding measurement.

14 Magazines are very good at figuring out who is physically attractive for cover shots; a financial magazine would be hard pressed to say any stock is obviously risky and consistent with standard theory.

15 Pink (2011).

16 In *The General Theory*, Keynes compared risk taking to working in "smelly" occupations, noting such activity would require a premium. That is obviously wrong.

17 In the United States, Medal of Honor recipients brave death on the battlefield, usually risking probable death to save others.

18 John Campbell. "Asset Pricing at the Millennium," *The Journal of Finance*, 55 no. 4 (2000): 1515–1567.

19 Factor loading derived from covariances (the how much) and a risk premium on that factor (its price), generating a linear relation between risk and return.

20 This significantly lagged the broader market's 133 percent return over that same period.

21 See Staffcentrix website.

22 DALBAR (2011): "Quantitative Analysis of Investor Behavior." See www.dalbar.com.

23 Fama and French (1996) call the CAPM "empirically vacuous." Ross (1993) noted "having a low, middle or high beta does not matter; the expected return is the same."

24 The axioms were completeness, transitivity, continuity, and independence.

25 H. Levy and H.M. Markowitz. "Approximating Expected Utility by a Function of Mean and Variance," *American Economic Review* (June 1979). They noted that mean-variance optimization is an excellent approximation to expected utility when not normal.

26 In Cervantes' *Don Quixote*, part I, book 3, chapter 9, Sancho Panza stated, "'Tis the part of a wise man to keep himself today for tomorrow, and not venture all his eggs in one basket."

27 In the book of *Ecclesiastes*, which was written in approximately 935 B.C.: But divide your investments among many places,

for you do not know what risks might lie ahead.
in Shakespeare's *Merchant of Venice,*

> My ventures are not in one bottom trusted,
> Nor to one place; nor is my whole estate
> Upon the fortune of this present year:
> Therefore, my merchandise makes me not sad.

28 The expected return is simply proportional to the relative weighting on the risky portfolio.

$$E\left(R_i\right) = \left(1-z\right)R_f + zE(R_p)$$

This is easy, expected values are linear operators, so one can avoid correlations in determining an expected value. Now, because the risk-free asset has zero correlation and zero volatility, it can be ignored in the portfolio volatility estimation, and the volatility of the composite portfolio is even simpler; it is merely a function of the volatility of the portfolio of risk assets.

$$StDev\left(R_i\right) = z \cdot StDev(R_p)$$

That is, the volatility of the composite portfolio is merely a weighting of one's investment in the risky portfolio. Solving for z, we get

$$z = \frac{StDev(R_i)}{StDev(R_p)}$$

Plugging back into equation at the beginning, we get

$$R_i = \left(1 - \frac{StDev(R_i)}{StDev(R_p)}\right)R_f + \frac{StDev(R_i)}{StDev(R_p)}R_p$$

or

$$R_i = R_f + \frac{StDev\left(R_i\right)}{StDev\left(R_p\right)}(R_p - R_f)$$

This is the line generated from the risk-free asset, R_f through the portfolio of risky assets, R_p. The slope of which is maximized when $\frac{(R_p - R_f)}{StDev(R_p)}$ is maxi mized, and this is also called the Sharpe ratio. As a higher slope leads to a higher utility curve, this implies that the risky portfolio with the highest Sharpe ratio is the optimal risky portfolio.

29 Sharpe, 425–442. J. Linter. "The Valuation of Risk Assets and the Selection of Risky Investments in Stock Portfolios and Capital Budgets," *Review of Economics and Statistics* 47 no. 1 (1965): 13–37. J. Mossin. "Equilibrium in a Capital Asset Market," *Econometrica* 34 no. 4 (1966): 768–783. J. Treynor and K. Mazuy. "Can Mutual Funds Outguess the Market," *Harvard Business Review* 44 no. 4 (1966): 131–136.

30 The basic proof goes something like this. Everyone is optimizing their portfolio's utility, meaning they have solved the maximization problem for maximizing their mean return minus a linear function of their expected portfolio variance. A principle of optimization is that this implies that for every asset within the portfolio, the following first-order condition holds:

$$E(R_i) - a\sigma_{im} = k$$

Every asset has the same marginal value, taking into account that an asset's covariance is all that matters in a diversified portfolio. This is from the fact that for a large diversified portfolio, only covariance matters (σ_{im}). Holding undi-versifiable risk is inefficient and so not done. Regardless of the individual's risk preference (i.e., a), this equation holds for all assets for any particular investor.

$$E(R_f) - a\sigma_{fm} = k \ \rightarrow \ R_f = k$$

Now, given this applies also to the risk-free asset, this means that the risk-free asset's expected return is k. This is helpful because previously k was some unidentified parameter, whereas now it is some observable.

The next trick is to apply the equation to the market, that is, the covariance of the market with itself. This generates the following:

$$E(R_m) - a\sigma_m^2 = k \ \rightarrow \ a = \frac{E(R_m) - R_f}{\sigma_m^2} E(R_m)$$

Wow. Now, we have the unobserved parameter a as a function of observables. Plugging in for k and a, we now have

$$E(R_i) - \frac{E(R_m) - R_f}{\sigma_m^2} \sigma_{im} = R_f$$

Rearranging, we get

$$E(R_i) = R_f + \frac{\sigma_{im}}{\sigma_m^2}(E(R_m) - R_f)$$

Now, the ratio of the covariance over the variance we will call beta because this is the coefficient in an OLS regression of R_i on R_m (often called betas in introductory econometric courses). So we have

$$E(R_i) = R_f + \beta_i(E(R_m) - R_f)$$

31 Stephen Ross. "An Empirical Investigation of the Arbitrage Pricing Theory," *Journal of Finance* 35 no. 5 (1980): 1073–1103.

32 Fama (1991), 1575–1617.

33 Chen, Roll, Ross (1996), 383.

34 K.J. Arrow. and G. Debreu. "Existence of an Equilibrium for a Competitive Economy," *Econometrica* 22 (1954): 265–290.

35 Michael Harrison and David Kreps. "Martingales and arbitrage in multi-period securities markets," *Journal of Economic Theory* 20 (979): 381–408.

36 Rubinstein (1974), 225–244.

37 A dollar today can be transformed into X dollars tomorrow via an investment. The utility of a dollar today is the marginal utility of a dollar, based on how wealthy we are and other factors. The utility of a dollar tomorrow is the marginal utility of a dollar given how wealthy we are then. Let r represent the rate of return on the asset. The marginal value of a dollar today equals the product of the marginal value of a dollar tomorrow times the marginal value of a dollar tomorrow:

$$U_0' = U_1'(1 + r)$$

Here U_0' is the marginal value of a dollar today, and U_1' is the marginal value of a dollar tomorrow (they are primed because they are derivatives with respect to the input, usually a return or consumption). Today is represented by the subscript 0, tomorrow 1, the ' superscript notes this is the derivative of utility, or marginal utility, at that time.

$$1 = \frac{U_1'}{U_0'}(1+r)$$

Replacing $\frac{U_1'}{U_0'}$ with M, and $1+r$ with R, we get

$$1 = E[MR]$$

In the literature call the discount factor M for historical reasons ($M = DF$). Tricky thing is that because M and R are random variables, they obey this following statistical law:

$$E[MR] = E[M]E[R] + cov(M, R)$$

Which can be rearranged to

$$E[R_i] = \frac{1}{E[M]} - \frac{cov(M, R_i)}{E[M]}$$

Now, here's where the algebra becomes interesting. Assume we are considering a risk-free asset. It has no variance so no covariance (i.e., covariance with anything is zero). So this nails down $E[M]$:

$$E[R_f] = R_f = \frac{1}{E[M]}$$

The value of a dollar tomorrow is negatively correlated with the expected market return given the concavity of utility (higher wealth means we are richer and thus value money less), the value of a dollar tomorrow is, therefore, negatively correlated with the return on the stock market. If the economy has a representative agent with a well-defined utility function, then the SDF is related to the marginal utility of aggregate consumption. So replace U_i' with $-\gamma R_i$, so now

$$M = \frac{U_1'}{U_0'} = \frac{-\gamma R_i}{U_0'}$$

Now we already know that by definition, $M = \frac{U_1'}{U_0'}$ so replacing M with these equations we get

$$E[R_i] = \left(\frac{U_0'}{U_1'}\right)\left(\frac{cov(R_m, R_i)}{U_0'}\right)$$

Crossing out the U_0's, we have

$$E[R_i] = R_f + \frac{\gamma cov(R_m, R_i)}{U_1'}$$

Apply this equation to the market itself so that, $R_i = R_m$

$$E[R_m] = R_f + \frac{\gamma cov(R_m, R_m)}{U_1'}$$

Then the marginal value of a dollar today is worth

$$U_1' = \frac{\gamma \sigma_m^2}{E[R_m - R_f]}$$

Given the above, we can replace the denominator and have

$$E[R_i] = R_f + E[R_m - R_f]\frac{cov(R_m, R_i)}{\sigma_m^2}$$

Which given the definition of β is merely the CAPM equation

$$E(R) = R + \beta E(R - R)$$

QED

38 M. Lettau and S Ludvigson. "Consumption, Aggregate Wealth, and Expected Stock Returns," *The Journal of Finance* 56 no. 3 (001) :815–849.

39 M.C. Jensen. "The Performance of Mutual Funds in the Period 1945–64," *Journal of Finance* 23 no. 2 (1968): 389–416. J. Treynor and K. Mazuy. "Can Mutual Funds Outguess the Market," *Harvard Business Review*, 44 no. 4 (1966): 131–136. William F. Sharpe. "Mutual Fund Performance," *Journal of Business* 39 no. 1 (1966): 119–138.

40 Douglas (1969), 3–45.

41 This unpublished work was noted by Douglas in his paper.

42 Correctly, one would properly say "not rejecting the CAPM null hypothesis," and that's what I mean here.

43 October 16, 1990 press release. The Royal Swedish Academy of Sciences. The Sveriges Riksbank Prize in Economic Sciences in Memory of Alfred Nobel 1990.

44 See Engle's 1984 classic on the subject, and note he was later rewarded with a Nobel Prize. These kind of distinctions were considered the essence of good finance in the 1980s. Robert F. Engle. "Wald, Likelihood Ratio, and Lagrange Multiplier Tests in Econometrics," In M.D. Intriligator and Z. Griliches, eds., *Handbook of Econometrics* II (Elsevier), 796–801.

45 Rolf Banz. "The Relationship Between Return and Market Value of Common Stocks," *Journal of Financial Economics* 9 no. 1 (1981): 3–18. M.R. Reinganum. "Misspecification of Capital Asset Pricing: Empirical Anomalies Based on Earnings Yields and Market Values, *Journal of Financial Economics* 9 no. 1 (1981): 19–46.

46 *Journal of Financial Economics*, 1983, v12.

47 Tyler Shumway and Vince Warther. "The Delisting Bias in CRSP's Nasdaq Data and Its Implications for the Size Effect," *Journal of Finance* 54 (1999): 2361–2379.

48 Peter Bernstein. "Most Nobel Minds, *CFA Magazine* (Nov-Dec 2005).

49 R. Roll. "A Critique of the Asset Pricing Theory's Tests: Part I: On Past and Potential Testability of the Theory," *Journal of Financial Economics* 4 no. 2 (1977): 129–176.

50 See Levy, Post, and van Vliet (2008).

51 Roll (1977), 129–176.

52 Gregory Connor and Robert A. Korajczyk. "Factor Models in Portfolio and Asset Pricing Theory." In John Guerard, ed., *Handbook of Portfolio Construction: Contemporary Applications of Markowitz Techniques* (London: Springer, 2010), 410–418. SSRN: http://ssrn.com/abstract=1139062.

53 Fama and French (1993, 1995), Jegadeesh and Titman (1993) used the value-weighted index; Chopra, Lakonishok, and Ritter (1992), Jones (1993) used the equal-weighted; and Kothari, Shanken, and Sloan (1995) used both.

54 Fama and French (1992), 427–467.

55 S.A. Ross. "Is Beta Useful?" In *The CAPM Controversy: Policy and Strategy Implications for Investment Management* (Charlottesville, NC: AIMR, 1993). What is really interesting is that Ross was then famous for promoting the APT theory that had the CAPM beta as its most intuitive and statistically important factor, so if the CAPM betas did not have explanatory power you would think he could have mentioned this earlier.

56 Fama, French, and Davis (2000) shot back that their approach did work better on the early, smaller sample and the more survivorship biased 1933–1960 period, but that implies at best that size and value seem the essence of characteristics, not factors, over the more recent and better documented 1963–2000 period. Data in favor of Daniel and Titman's characteristics approach were found in France by Souad Ajili (2003) and in Japan by Daniel, Titman, and Wei (2001). In a similar vein, Todd Houge and Tim Loughran (2006) found mutual funds with the highest loadings on the value factor reported no return premium over the same 1975–2002 period, even though the value factor generated a 6.2 percent average annual return over the same period. Loading on the factor alone did not generate a return premium.

57 See Dichev (1998); Campbell, Hilscher, and Szilagyi (2006); Distressed firms have much higher volatility, market betas, and loadings on value and small-cap risk factors than stocks with a low risk of failure; furthermore, they have much worse performance in recessions. See Opler and Titman (1995).

58 Q. Dai and K.J. Singleton. "Expectation Puzzles, Time-Varying Risk Premia, and Affine Models of the Term Structure," *Journal of Financial Economics* 63 no. 3 (2002): 415–441.

59 Jagannathan Wang (1996), 3–53.

60 The first paragraph of my dissertation is as follows: "This paper documents two new facts. First, over the past 30 years variance has been

negatively correlated with expected return for NYSE & AMEX stocks and this relationship is not accounted for by several well-known prespecified factors (e.g., the price-to-book ratio or size). More volatile stocks have lower returns, other things equal. In fact, one of the prespecified factors, size, obscures this inverse relationship. Second, I document that open-end mutual funds have strong preferences for stocks that are liquid, well-known, and most interestingly, highly volatile stocks." See www.efalken.com/papers/efdiss94.pdf.

61 Andrew Ang, R.J. Hodrick, Y. Xing, and X. Zhang. The Cross-Section of Volatility and Expected Returns, *The Journal of Finance* 61 no. 1 (2006): 259–299. Andrew Ang, Joseph Chen, and Yuhang Xing. Downside Risk, *Review of Financial Studies* 19 no. 4 (2006): 1191–1239.

62 Ronnie Shah. "Understanding Low Volatility Strategies: Minimum Variance." Dimensional Fund Advisors white paper, 2011.
Bernd Scherer. "A New Look at Minimum Variance Investing" (2010). Available at SSRN: http://ssrn.com/abstract=1681306.

63 Schwartz (2000), Clarke, de Silva and Thorley (2006), Blitz and van Vliet (2007)

64 See www.betaarbitrage.com.

65 C.S. Jones. "Extracting Factors from Heteroskedastic Asset Returns," *Journal of Financial Economics* 62 no. 2 (2001): 293–325. Gregory Connor and Robert A. Korajczyk. "A Test for the Number of Factors in an Approximate Factor Model," *Journal Of Finance* 48 (1993): 1263–1263.

66 T. Shumway. "The Delisting Bias in Crisp Data, *Journal of Finance* 52 (1997): 327–340.
T. Shumway and Vince Warther. "The Delisting Bias in CRSP's Nasdaq Data and Its Implications for the Size Effect, *Journal of Finance*, 54 (1997): 2361–2379.

67 Andrea Frazzin and Lasse Heje Pedersen. "Betting against Beta," NBER Working Paper Series, Vol. w16601 (2010). SSRN: http://ssrn.com/abstract=1723048. Enrico G. De Giorgi, Thierry Post, and Atakan Yalcin. "A Concave Security Market Line" (2012). Available at SSRN: http://ssrn.com/abstract=1800229.

68 See Frazzini and Pedersen. 2011. Betting Against Beta. SSRN: http://ssrn.com/abstract=1723048

69 Dichev, 1998. The Altman model is popular in large part because it is so easy to make a better model, so it's the main model used to benchmark one's newer model.

70 F. Modigliani and M. Miller. "The Cost of Capital, Corporation Finance and the Theory of Investment, *American Economic Review* 48 no. 3 (1958): 261–297.

71 This was also in Robert A. Haugen and Nardin L. Baker. "Commonality in the Determinants of Expected Stock Returns, *Journal of Financial Economics* 41 no. 3 (1996): 401–439.

72 Knightian uncertainty is that which cannot be quantified into an actuarial expectation, as with the popping of Champaign bottles in inventory, and was exposited in Frank Knight's book *Risk, Uncertainty, and Profit* (1921). Ellsberg (1961) noted that people behaved differently when given urns with balls that contain specific amounts of red and blue, versus those that contained balls that contained either black or yellow balls. This is aversion to incomplete information. The risky prospect is perceived as more justifiable than the ambiguous one because potentially available probabilistic information is missing from the ambiguous urn.

73 Jay Ritter. "Returns on IPOs during the Five Years after Issuing, for IPOs from 1970–2009" (2011). See http://bear.warrington.ufl.edu/ritter/IPOs2010-5yearsMay2011.pdf.

74 The CBS weekly show *60 Minutes* had a story on November 13, 2011, by Steve Kroft on congressional stock trading, and mentioned Nancy Pelosi had access to ten IPOs in her career. IPOs average a 12% return their first day of trading. That's ten more than I've had.

75 Here are some: Robert Jones and Russ Wermers. "Active Management in Mostly Efficient Markets," *Financial Analysts Journal* (Nov/Dec 2011): 29–45. Robert Kosowski, Allan Timmermann, Russ Wermers, and Hal White. "Can Mutual Fund 'Stars' Really Pick Stocks? New Evidence from a Bootstrap Analysis," *Journal of Finance* (2006): 2551–2595. Russ Wermers. "Mutual Fund Performance: An Empirical Decomposition into Stock-Picking Talent, Style, Transactions Costs, and Expenses," *The Journal of Finance* 55 no. 4 (2000): 1655–1703. Russ Wermers, Russ. "Performance Evaluation with Portfolio Holdings Information," *North American Journal of Economics and Finance* (2006): 207–230.

76 There are many papers on both sides. See Bansal and Lundblad (2002) for a positive relationship between the expected excess market return and

conditional variance, whereas Glosten, Jagannathan, and Runkle (1993) find the opposite.

77 Benjamin Graham and Jason Zweig. *The Intelligent Investor*, revised 1973 edition, (New York: HarperBusiness Essentials, 2003).

78 Ben S. Branch and Aixin Ma. "The Overnight Return, One More Anomaly" (September 6, 2006). SSRN: http://ssrn.com/abstract=937997.
Zvi Wiener and Robert George Tompkins. "Bad Days and Good Nights: A Re-Examination of Non-Traded and Traded Period Returns (March 4, 2008). SSRN: http://ssrn.com/abstract=1102165.

79 For this adjusted mid price, I calculated as (bestbidSize*ask+bestAskSize* bid)/(BestBidSize+BestAskSize).

80 See Jay Ritter. "Economic Growth and Equity Returns," *Pacific-Basin Finance Journal*, 13 (2005): 489-503.

81 See Ivo Welch. *Corporate Finance: An Introduction* (New York: Prentice Hall, 2010). For average practitioners, see Pablo Fernandez, Javier Aguirreamalloa, and Luis Avendaño. "Equity Market Risk Premium Used in 56 Countries in 2011: A Survey with 6,014 Answers (July 25, 2011). Available at SSRN: http://ssrn.com/abstract=1898186.

82 See Ivo Welch. "A Note on the Equity Size Puzzle," Anderson Graduate School Working Paper.

83 "Always go too far, because that's where you'll find the truth." —Albert Camus

84 William Goetzmann and Nadav Peles. "Cognitive Dissonance and Mutual Fund Investors," *Journal of Financial Research*, 20 no. 2 (1997): 145–158. Markus Glaser and Martin Weber. "Why Inexperienced Investors Do Not Learn: They Do Not Know Their Past Portfolio Performance," *Finance Research Letters* 4 no. 4 (2007): 203–216.

85 T.A. Rietz. "The Equity Risk Premium: A Solution," *Journal of Monetary Economics* 22 no. 1 (1988): 117–131.

86 S.W. Brown, W. Goetzmann, R. Ibbotson, and S. Ross. "Survivorship Bias in Performance Studies," *Review of Financial Studies* 5 (1992): 553–580. Robert J. Barro. (2006): Rare Disasters And Asset Markets In The Twentieth Century, *The Quarterly Journal of Economics* 121 no. 3 (2006): 823–866.

87 Alice Hanson Jones. *American Colonial Wealth* (New York: Arno Press, 1977).

88 William G. Schwert. "Indexes of United States Stock Prices from 1802 to 1987," *Journal of Business* 63 (1990): 399–426.

89 Kay Giesecke, Francis A. Longstaff, Stephen M. Schaefer, and Ilya A. Strebulaev. "Corporate Bond Default Risk: A 150-Year Perspective" (March 2010). NBER Working Paper Series, Vol. w15848.

90 Jeremy Siegel. *Stocks for the Long Run* (New York: McGraw-Hill, 1998).

91 Niall J. Gannon and Michael J. Blum. "After-Tax Returns on Stocks Versus Bonds for the High Tax Bracket Investor," *The Journal Of Wealth Management* 9 no. 2 (2006): 35-45. .

92 Brad M. Barber and Terrance Odean. "Trading Is Hazardous to Your Wealth: The Common Stock Investment Performance of Individual Investors," *Journal of Finance*, 55 no. 2 (2000): 773–806.

93 Ilia Dichev. "What Are Stock Investors Actual Historical Returns? Evidence from Dollar Weighted Returns," *American Economic Review*, 97 (2007): 386–401.

94 Barber and Odean (2000), 773–806.

95 Charles M. Jones. Charles M. (2002): "A Century of Stock Market Liquidity and Trading Costs" (2002). Available at SSRN: http://ssrn.com/abstract=313681 or doi:10.2139/ssrn.313681.

96 "Moral Hazard" is the risk that the presence of a contract will affect on the behavior of one or more parties. The classic example is in the insurance industry, where coverage against a loss might increase the risk-taking behavior of the insured.

97 T.J. Moskowitz and A. Vissing-Jorgensen. "The Returns to Entrepreneurial Investment: A Private Equity Premium Puzzle?" *American Economic Review* 92 no. 4 (2002): 745–778.

98 J. Heaton and D. Lucas. "Portfolio Choice and Asset Prices: The Importance of Entrepreneurial Risk," *The Journal of Finance* 55 no. 3 (2000):1163–1198.

99 Antti Ilmanen. *Expected Returns: An Investor's Guide to Harvesting Market Rewards* (New York: Wiley, 2011).

100 Jianping Mei and Michael Moses. "Wealth Management for Collectors," *Journal of Investment Consulting*, 11 no. 1 (2010): 50–59. Available at SSRN: http://ssrn.com/abstract=1691267.

101 Robert J. Hodrick. *The Empirical Evidence on the Efficiency of Forward and Futures Foreign Exchange Markets* (Chur, Switzerland: Harwood, 1987).

102 Markus K. Brunnermeier, Stefan Nagel, and Lasse H. Pedersen. "Carry Trades and Currency Crashes." In *NBER Macro Annual* (University of Chicago Press, 2008.)

103 F. Black. "The Pricing of Commodity Contracts," *Journal of Financial Economics*, 3 (1976): 167–169.

104 Gary B. Gorton and K. Geert Rouwenhorst. (2006): "Facts and Fantasies about Commodity Futures," *Financial Analysts Journal* (March/April 2006): 47–68.

105 Dove Foundation, "Profitability Study of MPAA-Rated Movies" (2005). http://www.dove.org/research/DoveFoundationROI-Study2005.pdf.

106 Vanguard Investments. "Hedge Fund Index Biases" (November 2004).

107 The VAN Companies. "Historical Hedge Fund Returns Fairly Represent Performance" (January 2005). Commentary by George P. Van, Zhiyi Song.

108 See Simon Lack. *Hedge Fund Mirage* (Wiley, 2012)

109 $E(-\exp(-ax)) = \text{mean}(x) - a \cdot \text{Variance}(x)/2$ when x is normally distributed.

110 The paper does use the phrase *catching* and not *keeping* because in this model prior aggregate consumption is the benchmark. The common phrase uses *keeping*.

111 John Maynard Keynes. "The General Theory of Employment," *Quarterly Journal of Economics* 51 (1937): 209–223.

112 The key difference between Keynes and Knight was not their conception of risk but rather the implication. For Keynes and his followers, the subjectivity of risk was key to business cycles because it could shift without much actually happening, as these beliefs were never objective in any way to begin with. Animal spirits might move around and then be stuck in a pessimistic depression. For Knight, the uncertainty of risk was the essence of profitability because although an arbitrage can actuarially sound probabilities, for one-off cases that are used in most businesses, such events cannot be arbitraged. The revival of Minsky after the 2008 financial crisis has highlighted this different conception of risk, uncertainty.

113 Xavier Gabaix. "Variable Rare Disasters: A Tractable Theory of Ten Puzzles in Macro-Finance," *American Economic Review Papers and Proceedings*, 98 no. 2 (2008): 64–67.

114 A similar paper was earlier done by Pesendorfer (1995), who found a status-oriented utility function can be an efficient signaling device because status goods signal ability. In sum, status seeking is an evolutionarily stable strategy.

115 Pit vipers have infrared "vision" that captures wavelengths from 5–30 nm, and though photoreceptors detect light via photochemical reactions, the protein in the pits of snakes is a heat-sensitive ion channel.

116 L. Young, J. Camprodon, M. Hauser, A. Pascual-Leone, and R. Saxe. (2010). "Disruption of the Right Temporo-Parietal Junction with Transcranial Magnetic Stimulation Reduces the Role of Beliefs in Moral Judgment." *PNAS* 107 no. 15 (2010): 6753–6758.

117 http://en.wikipedia.org/wiki/Checker_shadow_illusion

118 Giacomo Rizzolatti and Laila Craighero. "The Mirror-Neuron System," *Annual Review of Neuroscience* 27 (2004): 169–192.

119 David Rock. "Managing with the Brain in Mind," *Strategy+ Business* 56 (2009). Available at http://www.strategy-business.com/article/09306?gko=5df7f.

120 Mark, Pagel. *Wired for Culture: Origins of the Social Mind* (W.W. Norton & Company, 2011).

121 Economists such as Dan Ariely (2008) noted that the complexity of calculations leads many people to borrow from the wisdom of crowds and use peers for benchmarking.

122 Dan Brown. *Human Universals* (New York: McGraw-Hill, 1991).

123 Michael Marmot. *The Status Syndrome* (New York: Times Books, 2004).

124 The others should be obvious, but Keynes talked a lot about this in his "Economics of Our Grandchildren" (1930) essay.

125 D. Knight, J. and Song, L. (2006). *Subjective well-being and its determinants in rural China.* University of Nottingham, University of Nottingham, mimeo.

126 Robert Frank. *The Darwin Economy: Liberty, Competition, and the Common Good* (Princeton University Press, 2011).

127 K. Fliessbach, B. Weber, P. Trautner, T. Dohmen, U. Sunde, C.E. Elger, and A. Falk. "Social Comparison Affects Reward-Related Brain Activity in the Human Ventral Striatum," *Science* 318 no. 5854 (2007): 1305–1308.

128 David Graeber. *Debt: The First 5,000 Years* (New York: Melville House, 2010).

129 The ! implies one must make a click sound before the k, which is not common for English, thus the special character.

130 In Friedrich Durrenmatt's novel *Traps*, which involves a seemingly innocent man put on trial by a group of retired lawyers for a mock trial game, the man inquires what his crime shall be. "An altogether minor matter," the prosecutor says, "a crime can always be found."

131 P. Tanous. *Investment Gurus* (New York: Prentice Hall, 1998).

132 Ibid.

133 Bernstein (2005), 36–43.

134 Aristotle, Nicomedian Ethics.

135 Reminds one of Oscar Wilde's comment, "One can always be kind to people about whom one cares nothing."

136 Plato, see the dialogues Protagoras and Meno.

137 Jeremy Siegel. *Stocks for the Long Run: A Guide to Selecting Markets for Long-term Growth* (Burr Ridge, IL: Irwin Professional Publishing, 1994).

138 A. Dreber, C.L. Apicella, D.T.A. Eisenberg, J.R. Garcia, R. Zamore, J.K. Lum, and B.C. Campbell. "The 7R Polymorphism in the Dopamine Receptor D4 Gene (DRD4) Is Associated with Financial Risk-Taking in Men," *Evolution and Human Behavior* 30 no. 2 (2008): 85–92.

139 De Long, Shleifer, Summers, and Waldmann, 1990, 703–738.

140 New York Times. "NBA Players Make Their Way Back to College" (October 5, 2009). Available at http://www.nytimes.com/2009/10/06/sports/basketball/06nba.html.

141 One could argue that even though a lot went bankrupt, some did exceptionally well, so the average is actually quite good. Although possible, I doubt the data reflect that scenario.

142 G-loading is the single factor that tends to explain individual differences across different mental tests. IQ tests are generally thought of as trying to maximize a g-loading. See Shane Frederick. "Cognitive Reflection and Decision Making," *Journal of Economic Perspectives*, 19 no. 4 (2005): 25–42.

143 Mark Grinblatt, Matti Keloharju, and Juhani Linnainmaa. "IQ and Stock Market Participation," *Journal of Finance* 66 no. 6 (2011): 2121–2164.

144 Pink (2011).

145 T.S. Ferguson. "Who Solved the Secretary Problem?" *Statistical Science* 4 no. 3 (1989): 282–296.

146 One of the wisest things Hyman Minsky ever told me was not to think I knew everything until I was at least thirty. I thought the old man was crazy because thirty was ancient. With hindsight as a forty-six-year-old, I consider even my thirty-year-old self pretty ignorant.

147 Roy Baumeister. *Is There Anything Good About Men?: How Cultures Flourish by Exploiting Men* (Oxford University Press, 2010).

148 Robert J. Aumann. "Rule Rationality vs. Act Rationality" (2008). Third Meeting in Economics Sciences, Nobel Laureate Meetings at Lindau.

149 A good example is warblers, which are reasonably discerning in detecting impostor eggs using subtle cues, but once hatched, apply the rule "feed every open mouth" without any discretion.

150 Peter L. Bossaerts. *The Paradox of Asset Pricing* (Princeton University Press, 2002).

151 D. Frisch and J. Baron. "Ambiguity and Rationality," *Journal of Behavioral Decision Making* 1 (1988): 149–157.

152 Aragones et al. called "fact-free learning" the process of discovering the correct odds because they involve innumerable connections between events, and finding all the patterns is an NP-complete problem, meaning they are infinitely easier to confirm than discover. See Enriqueta Aragones, Itzhak Gilboa, Andrew Postlewaite, and David Schmeidler. "Fact-Free Learning," *American Economic Review* 95 no. 5 (2005): 1355–1368.

153 William Goetzmann and Alok Kumar. "Diversification Decisions of Individual Investors and Asset Prices" (2004). Yale School of Management Working Papers.

154 M.T. Bradshaw. "The Use of Target Prices to Justify Sell-Side Analysts' Stock Recommendations," *Accounting Horizons* 16 (2002): 27–42.

155 For example, Rex Sinquefeld, Eugene Fama.

156 See Claude Erb and Campbell R. Harvey. "The Tactical and Strategic Value of Commodity Futures," *Financial Analysts Journal* (January 12, 2006). Available at SSRN: http://ssrn.com/abstract=650923 or http://dx.doi.org/10.2139/ssrn.650923.

157 Different from the average portfolio not merely in "the factor loadings but in the many idiosyncratic strategies that people attempt.

158 Jay Ritter. "The Long-Run Performance of Initial Public Offerings," *Journal of Finance*, 46 no. 1 (1991): 3–27.

159 K.B. Diether, C.J. Malloy, and A. Scherbina. "Differences of Opinion and the Cross Section of Stock Returns," *The Journal of Finance* 57 no. 5 (2002): 2113–2141.

160 E. Miller. "Risk, Uncertainty, and Divergence of Opinion," Journal of Finance 32 no. 4 (1977): 1151–1168.

161 Svenson (1981), 143–148.

162 J. Haidt. *The Happiness Hypothesis: Finding Modern Truth in Ancient Wisdom* (New York: Basic Books, 2006).

163 Robert Trivers. *Folly of Fools: Deceit and Self-Deception* (New York: Basic Books, 2011).

164 Hilary Tindle, Yue-Fang Chang, Lewis H. Kuller, JoAnn E. Manson, Jennifer G. Robinson, Milagros C. Rosal, Greg J. Siegle, and Karen A. Matthews.

"Optimism, Cynical Hostility, and Incident Coronary Heart Disease and Mortality in the Women's Health Initiative, Epidemiology." (2009).

165 See Danny Kahneman. *Thinking Fast and Slow* (Allen Lane: 2011).

166 Satoshi Kanazawa. *The Intelligence Paradox* (John Wiley & Sons, 2012).

167 Strangely, Kahneman is a fan of Nassim Taleb's work, whose signature claim is that investors tend to prefer situations where they are in a sense selling out-of-the-money options or picking up pennies in front of a steam roller, enjoying the small gains in exchange for the occasional catastrophe. In this case we underweight small probability but large loss events.

168 Campbell Harvey and Akhtar Siddique. "Autoregressive Conditional Skewness," *Journal of Financial and Quantitative Analysis* 34 no. 4 (1999): 465–488; or A. Kraus and R. H. Litzenberger. "Skewness Preference and Valuation of Risk Assets," *Journal of Finance* 31 no. 4 (1976): 1085–1100.

169 See Section 4.14 on the equity risk premium.

170 Snowberg and Wolfers (2010), 723-745.

171 They note that if the risk-loving model is correct, one has the model
$$Pr(a) \cdot U(O(a)) = Pr(b) \cdot U(O(b))$$
where $O(a)$ is the odds (e.g., 10–1) of horse a winning. In contrast, in the misconception (stupidity) model, the implied relation is
$$Pr(a) \cdot (O(a)+1) = Pr(b) \cdot (O(b)+1) = 1$$

172 Falkenstein (1994), 111–135.

173 See http://pressroom.blogs.pace.edu/2011/10/20/news-release-academic-study-reveals-correlations-of-stock-prices-with-consumer-brand-fan-counts/.

174 E. Sirri and P. Tufano. "Costly Search and Mutual Fund Flows," *Journal of Finance* 53 (1998): 1589–1622.

175 'Sell' for Research Renegades Becomes Business Off Wall Street, *Bloomberg Magazine*, October 9, 2009.

176 See Kathryn Schulz. *Being Wrong: Adventures in the Margin of Error* (New York: Ecco/HarperCollins, 2010).

177 Unimportant: no interest in dissertation findings on low volatility or attempts to create low-volatility fund. Trivial, obvious, and wrong, were all criticisms in rejected journal submissions. Illegal: my old employer filed suit against me arguing that I should be enjoined from creating low-volatility portfolios because of my work with it at their shop.

178 From Douglas R. Hofstadter, *Mathemagical Themas* (Bantam Books, 1985): page 113.

179 One loses the "Independence of irrelevant alternatives," an axiom of decision theory that helps researchers model outcomes.

180 F.A. Hayek. "The Use of Knowledge in Society," *American Economic Review*, 35 no. 4 (1945): 519–553.

181 Robert Axelrod. "The Evolution of Strategies in the Iterated Prisoner's Dilemma." In Lawrence Davis, ed., *Genetic Algorithms and Simulated Annealing*. (London: Pitman, 1987), 32–41. R.L. Trivers. "The Evolution of Reciprocal Altruism," *Quarterly Review of Biology* 46 (1971): 35–57.

182 For example, Gazzaniga (2011) writes about experiments where they give a student an amphetamine, then expose the subject to a partner with a strong personality. For students who were unaware they received a stimulant, they were more likely to think they really disliked or like that person, cuing off their higher heart rate; for students aware they had ingested a stimulant, they were less moved by the actor. We can change our thoughts, especially when we better understand why we have the instinctual feelings we do have, towards people and ideas.

183 Charles Darwin. *Descent of Man* (1871), 385.

184 David Goodstein. *On Fact and Fraud: Cautionary Tales from the Front Lines of Science* (Princeton University Press, 2010). John Walley. *Einstein's Luck: The Truth behind Some of the Greatest Scientific Discoveries* (Oxford University Press, 2003). William Broad. "After 400 Years, A Challenge to Kepler: He Fabricated His Data, Scholar Says." *New York Times*, 23 January 1990.

185 See Michael S. Gazzaniga. "The Split Brain Revisited," *Scientific American* (July 1998).

186 In another example, Campbell Harvey, editor of the *Journal of Finance*, has on his website a nice picture with risk on the *x*-axis, and return on the *y*-axis. See http://web.archive.org/web/20110624024647/http://www.duke.edu/~charvey/Classes/ba350/history/history.htm No active researcher thinks that risk is synonymous with standard deviation anymore because the highest volatility stocks have the lowest returns, and mere volatility does not explain the cross-section of average returns for bonds, stocks, currencies, and commodities. Yet the graph implies this intuitive measure of risk shows the basic pricing relationship that presumably exists in all asset markets.

187 Jay Shanken and Clifford Smith. "Implications of Capital Markets Research for Corporate Finance," *Financial Management*, 25 no. 1 (1996): 98–104.

188 John Bogle long believed in the power of index funds, but it was not until he was the CEO of a fund complex that he could implement his idea for a retail index fund, and even then he dealt with a skeptical board and relied heavily on authority figures such as Paul Samuelson (other fund pioneers Rex Sinquefeld and Jack McQuown were also well-connected). Imagine if he were a bright-eyed young kid with merely a PowerPoint presentation and his own data. It is essential to have the right connections when you have a good idea, more so the bigger the idea.

189 My Falken Fund LLC generate a return of 12 percent above the S&P 500 from January 1997 through August 2001. Mainly because of out-performance from 2000 onward. The fund bought thirty large-cap stocks with below average volatility and the highest twelve–month prior return, rebalanced every six to twelve months. I stopped it as I became a portfolio manager within Deephaven, a hedge fund.

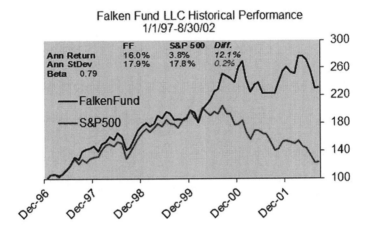

190 From David Hakes. "Confession of an Economist: Writing to Impress Rather than Inform," *Econ Journal Watch*, 6 no. 3 (2009): 349–51. Economist David Hakes shares this publishing anecdote:

"When we submitted the paper to risk, uncertainty, and insurance journals, the referees responded that the results were self-evident. After some degree of frustration, my coauthor suggested that the problem with the paper might be that we had made the argument too easy to follow, and thus referees and editors were not sufficiently impressed. He said that he could make the paper more impressive by generalizing the model. While making the same point as the original paper, the new paper would be more mathematically elegant, and it would become absolutely impenetrable to most readers. The resulting paper had fifteen equations, two propositions and proofs, dozens of additional mathematical expressions, and a mathematical appendix containing nineteen equations and even more mathematical expressions. I personally could no longer understand the paper and I could not possibly present the paper alone. The paper was published in the first journal to which we submitted."

191 Monetary amount mentioned in trial. See Motion hearing, file No. 27–CV-07–4832. July 19, 2007. State of Minnesota, County of Hennepin.

192 Ibid. At one point, my lawyer argued that the allegation was so undefined "[Mr. Falkenstein] sits at home every day, no one will hire him." The judge responded "Doesn't he golf?" after which the transcript notes: [laughter in courtroom].

193 Ibid. Now, some might say this lawyer for my adversary was exaggerating. In any case, it was a very costly lawsuit so its instigators must have perceived some value.

194 In terms of cumulative distribution functions F_A and F_B, A is second-order stochastically dominant over B if and only if the area under F_A from minus infinity to x is less than or equal to that under F_B from minus infinity to x for all real numbers x, with strict inequality at some x; that is, $\int_{-\infty}^{x}\left(F_B(t)-F_A(t)\right)dt \geq 0 \; \forall \, x$, equivalently, A dominates B in the second order if and only if $E_a U(x) > = E_b U(x)$ for all nondecreasing and concave utility functions U.

195 Antti Ilmanen gave me most of these examples in private correspondence.

196 The expected amortized expected loss could be wrong, but it was a good-faith estimate.

197 For legal reasons, I would never say anything more because that's clearly asking for a defamation suit.

198 Madoff's sales pitch was an investment strategy consisting of purchasing thirty to thirty-five S&P 100 stocks, most correlated to that index, and the sale of out-of-the-money calls on the index and the purchase of out-of-the-money puts on the index. To generate the returns, Madoff generated during his Ponzi scheme, he would have had to have generated more

volume than was in the market. Further, his beta was implausibly low for this strategy.

199 Gary Gorton. "The Big Short Shrift," *Journal of Economic Literature* (2011). Available at SSRN: http://ssrn.com/abstract=1768032.

200 In Jonathan Haidt's *The Happiness Hypothesis*, he describes our conscious selves as mainly confabulators for our desires. On a very fundamental level, we selectively present arguments and facts that support our prejudices. Jonathan Haidt. *The Happiness Hypothesis: Finding Modern Truth in Ancient Wisdom* (New York Basic Books, 2006).

201 Eric Falkenstein. *Finding Alpha: The Search for Alpha when Risk and Return Break Down*, (Hoboken, NJ: Wiley Finance, 2009).

202 In Keynes's 1930 essay "Economic Possibilities for our Grandchildren," he imagined several more generations of income growth would leave people mainly concerned with how to spend our leisure time.

203 Dale Carnegie was a pioneer of self-help books on improving one's attitude, happiness, and material success, with books like *How to Win Friends and Influence People*.

204 *Ikigai* is the purpose that gives people satisfaction and meaning, and is statistically related to happiness. The Serenity Prayer is as follows: God grant me the serenity to accept the things I cannot change; courage to change the things I can; and wisdom to know the difference.

205 Helumt Schoeck. *Envy* (Indianapolis, IN: Liberty Fund, 1987).

206 A snipe hunt is a charade adults play on children, usually at group camping events. One tells the children they are hunting snipe, and someone pretends to grab the snipe in a bag and feign fear and accomplishment. Then they tell the children it's just a toy animal, and everyone laughs (especially if a couple of the children cry). The snipe is just a mythical rodent of some sort.

207 For more, see Xavier Gabaix, Arvind Krishnamurthy, and Olivier Vigneron. "Limits of Arbitrage: Theory and Evidence from the Mortgage-Backed Securities Market," *The Journal of Finance*, 62 no. 2 (2007): 557–595. They make the following statement: "We establish three principal empirical results in the paper. First, we show that prepayment risk carries a positive risk premium. Second, we show that the observed covariance between prepayment risk and either aggregate wealth or consumption implies a sign that is opposite that required to match the observed prices of prepayment risk under traditional asset pricing theory. This suggests that the marginal investor in the MBS market is not the representative investor hypothesized

by the traditional CAPM or consumption-CAPM model." Such reasoning leads nowhere.

208 Hayek's essay *The Use of Knowledge in Society* mentions often the "use of time and place" meaning, the knowledge of someone with highly contextual, particular, I would say, parochial, knowledge.

Made in the USA
Charleston, SC
21 August 2012